NEVER STOP WALKING

A Wales Coast Path Adventure

Other titles by Jonathan Wunrow and published by *Life is Twisted Press*:

- *High Points: A Climber's Guide to Central America* (2012)
- *Adventure Inward: A Risk Taker's Book of Quotes* (2013)
- *High Points: A Climber's Guide to Central America,*
  Second Edition (2017)
- *High Points: A Climber's Guide to South America* (2018)

NEVER STOP WALKING

A Wales Coast Path Adventure

JONATHAN WUNROW

Life is Twisted Press
Bloomington, IN

ISBN (Print, color edition): 978- 978-1-7363870-0-9
ISBN (Print, black and white edition): 978- 978-1-7363870-2-3
ISBN (eBook): 978- 978-1-7363870-1-6

Printed in the United States of America

Cover design by Bri Bruce Productions
Front cover photo by Jonathan Wunrow, Hiking Day #48 on the
Wales Coast Path as it passes through Pembrokeshire Coast
National Park near Broadhaven

Life is Twisted Press
801 W. 9th Street
Bloomington, Indiana 47404
Email: jonwunrow@gmail.com

This book is dedicated to my dad who, until his last days, loved adventure, loved life, and loved my mom.

AND THIS IS WHY . . .

What we get from this adventure is just sheer joy. And joy is, after all, the end of life. We do not live to eat and make money. We eat and make money to be able to enjoy life. That is what life means, and what life is for.

George Leigh Mallory

The more you live, the less you die.   Janice Joplin

Probing the edges of what may be possible is the only thing I know how to do. It is too late now at my age to stop, not to do it. And more than anything—I am like a child—I would always be unhappy if I didn't try.

Reinhold Mesner

I'm glad I did it, partly because it was well worth it, and chiefly because I shall never have to do it again.

Mark Twain

TABLE OF CONTENTS

NEVER
STOP
WALKING

INTRODUCTION

Shw' mae (pronounced shoo-my) – Hello, how are you?

The Welsh language (*Cymraeg*) has been spoken continuously in Wales throughout recorded history, and is currently spoken by over a half-million residents of Wales. According to a Welsh government survey, "Language Use in 2013–15," 24 percent of people aged three and over were able to speak Welsh. Welsh Medium schools (bilingual and immersion) are popping up all over the country in a nationalized effort to increase the number of fluent speakers.

To my non-linguistically oriented mind, Welsh is a language that is full of words that have almost no vowels, such as *cwtch* (a hug), *gwdihw* (owl), *chwyrligwgan* (merry-go-round), and *twmffat* (idiot). And names of towns that can be exceedingly long, including *Rhoslannerchrugog* (a village in North Wales), *Ystradgynlais* (near Swansea), and of course the town with the longest name in the world, *Llanfairpwllgwyngyllgogerychwyrndrobwllllantysiliogogogoch* (a village on the Welsh island of Anglesey). It is no wonder that a Welsh military regiment serving in Bosnia, used Welsh for secure emergency communications, much like the Navajo Code Talkers of the Second World War. I apologize in advance for any misspellings of Welsh words that appear in this book. I did my best to decipher the location spelling that I wrote in my journal, and then cross referencing with maps of the areas.

Starting *Never Stop Walking: A Wales Coast Path Adventure* by talking about the Welsh language is a bit of a metaphor for how fiercely proud and independent the people that we met in Wales are. In 2017, my wife Leslie and I hiked the entire Wales Coast Path, that begins in the city of Chester, just south of Liverpool, and follows the undulating coast of Wales for 870 miles to the city of Chepstow in the south.

Just about every day of our seventy-three day hike we saw street and village signs written in the incomprehensible Welsh language. We met warm and friendly Welsh people who were eager to tell us about the long and rich history of the land. And we walked passed castles and forts that were a testament of the many battles and struggles to remain independent.

Walking through Wales is a great way to become immersed in the country and the people who live there. When the Wales Coast Path was officially opened in May of 2012, Wales became the largest country in the world with a continuous path around its entire coast. The 870 miles of unbroken coastal walking allowed us to experience the very best of Wales: stunning scenery, stirring history, picturesque seaside towns, sandy beaches, varied wildlife, remote landscape, historic castles, large industrial cities, and best off the Welsh people, language, and culture.

Never Stop Walking isn't a guidebook for hiking the trail. Rather, it is the story of our 2017 hike. The book is a print version of the journal I kept, written at the end of each day and transcribed verbatim from those handwritten pages. It describes the emotional and geographic ups and downs of our adventure, and hints at what is necessary to complete a two-month long-distance hike for anyone who is contemplating their own adventure.

There are a handful of trail guides for Wales Coast Path hikers that have been written over the last few years. Several of these guidebooks and websites are noted in the final section of this book. The most comprehensive set of guidebooks to the trail is the *Official Wales Coast Guidebooks* published by Northern Eye Books. We relied on this seven book series and its detailed trail descriptions and maps nearly every step of the way. They contain everything you need to plan and walk the route. We did not bring or need any other maps or guides for our hike. *Never Stop Walking* serves as a real-life reality check to the maps and trail descriptions found in these published guides, and is laid out in the same seven trail sections as those in *Official Wales Coast Guidebooks*.

Why Did We Do It?

Probably the most often asked question that we've been asked since finishing our hike is "Why did you do it?" When I recently asked Leslie this question, she replied, "Because Jon made me," and then continued, "I like a challenge. And the Wales Coast Path was 140 miles longer than the Southwest Coast Path that we hiked in 2015, and I loved that hike." She concluded, "I knew that once I started I wasn't going to stop until we got to the end."

For me, I always need to have an adventure or two waiting in the wings so that I have something to look forward to. In my normal daily life, I struggle with living in the moment. Not very Zen, I know. I am always thinking ahead, planning my next trip, scouring maps, organizing logistics, and trying to come up with adventure ideas that will be physically and emotionally challenging. Planning and engaging in adventures helps me feel more content with the long months in between trips. I know that this isn't what the Dalai Lama teaches, but it's just the way my brain is wired. My first long-distance hike was a through-hike of the 2,600-mile Pacific Crest Trail from Mexico to Canada in 1987. It took 28 years to get around to completing my second long-distance trek when

Leslie and I through-hiked the 630-mile Southwest Coast Path in England in 2015. I like adventures that have a defined beginning and end, and that offer an intense sense of satisfaction when completed. And most of all, long-distance hikes and canoe trips and extended mountain climbs force me to focus on my breathing, and the wind direction and speed, and the messages my body is sending. I'm forced to be in the moment.

How Did We Do It?

The Wales Coast Path offers hikers the opportunity for myriad day hikes, weekend trips, week-long section hikes, and of course through-hiking in one go. Not everyone has the time, energy, inclination, or life circumstances to walk the entire 870 miles all at once. We met several people on the trail who were hiking it in weekend or week-long sections over a year or over several years.

In terms of through-hiking, some hikers (probably younger and in better shape) finish the trail in six or seven weeks, averaging over 20 miles a day. We took 10 and a half weeks, and even at that we walked every single one of the 73 days we were on the trail. Guidebooks suggest taking 12 or more weeks if you really want to fully enjoy the wildlife, scenery, history, and people.

Regardless of how long you plan for your hike to take, remember that the Wales Coast Path is a challenging route with plenty of rough ground, narrow paths, inclement weather, and lots of up-and-downs. You should allow extra time for the unexpected, like having to hole up in bad weather, to nurse blisters or strains back to health, to replace your blown-out hiking shoes, or buy the warm hat you forgot or the raincoat that you lost somewhere back on the trail.

The biggest decision that a through-hiker needs to make, other than how many weeks it will take to finish and the average number of miles to hike each day, is whether to camp or find indoor lodging every evening. In this day and age, there are lots of options for ultra-light tents, backpacks, sleeping bags and pads, stoves, and cooking gear. But making the decision to camp every night or most nights is an all-or-nothing proposition. If you are going to camp along the way, you pretty much need to either bring all of this stuff, or none of it. Which, even with the lightest of ultra-light gear, means adding 20-plus pounds to the clothes, electronics, raingear, water, book, journal, and miscellaneous sundries that you'll already be carrying. And Wales (and the United Kingdom in general) isn't really set up for tent camping like one would experience in the States.

It is definitely possible to plan your Wales Coast Path hike by staying in the countless hotels, B&Bs, guesthouses, and hostels located on the coast of Wales. Oftentimes, this means planning to call a taxi or take a local bus or train to get from a trail juncture to your lodging. And, at least during peak tourist season of July through early September, calling ahead to make a reservation. This is obviously the more expensive option over camping, but the reward of having a hot shower and a warm, dry bed at the end of a long, cold, rainy hike is worth saving up for.

When Did We Do It?

Early summer (May/June) in Wales is ideal for walking. Mid-summer (July/August) is the busiest tourist season with schools on holidays, crowded beaches, and lodging that can be hard to find, particularly on the northern coast. By September, most visitors have left for home, and you'll have the path largely to yourself. October starts to get chilly. We hiked from August 20th to November 2nd.

What the Guidebooks Don't Tell You

I am publishing this book for two primary reasons. The first is so that our kids and grandkids have something they can go back to in future years that will remind them of what their parents and grandparents were like—and maybe inspire them to create adventures of their own. The second reason is to offer potential Wales Coast Path hikers a sense of what it's really like to hike this amazing long-distance footpath. Also, I want to share a bit about the things the official guidebooks and websites don't include: stories about the people we met, the weather we hiked through, and the incredible scenery that surrounded us.

It is rare to find someone that you can adventure with for 24 hours a day for weeks or months at a time, through all kinds of challenges and hardships, and still like each other by the end. Leslie and I have now completed two long-distance hikes together, and for me they have probably provided the best moments of our marriage. Over the course of this hike, we were able to get into a kind of relationship rhythm, and sync, that only comes from experiencing every moment together for days and weeks in a row. Leslie would never describe herself as a hiker, but after through-hiking the Southwest Coast Path and the Wales Coast Path, I think she qualifies.

When we started our Wales Coast Path hike, Leslie and I decided that we would each keep a journal of the trip. Our idea (maybe in retrospect it was my idea) was that we'd each record our thoughts and feelings from our own perspectives, and then after the trip, we'd compare our points of view. Would there be a difference between how a man and a woman view the same events? What kinds of things would we each see as highlights, and low points, of the day? What will she pay attention to and find important enough to write about? What about me? It would be a psychological experiment in real time. After each of my daily journal entries, I have added Leslie's journal entries. You'll see right away that she is funnier than me, much less wordy, and a great observer of people.

These are just a few of the reasons why I loved almost every minute of this adventure with Leslie, why I'm already planning our next long-distance hike together, and why I love her so much! You can decide for yourself how our psychological experiment turned out.

Happy Hiking!

- Jonathan Wunrow, November 2020

SECTION ONE:
NORTH WALES COAST

Chester to Bangor

Sunday, August 20, 2017

Potential titles for this journal and future best-selling book about our upcoming hike:

The Whales go to Wales
Two Whales Walking
Whales Hike Wales
Whales: A Hiker's Guide to the Wales Coast Path
Whales Gone Wild

These possible book titles are born from the fact that I am feeling overweight, to the tune of 25 pounds, and Leslie says she is feeling the same way. Hence, the "whale" metaphor. We both are earnestly hoping that after hiking around 900 miles, we will meet our weight-loss goals. We'd better. Leslie did some online calculations based on averaging 12 miles per day of hiking and eating lots of food every day, we should still lose a pound every four days or so. *Should.*

It is Sunday, around 12:30pm. We're on a train speeding from Euston Station in London to Crewe. Neither of us have any idea where Crewe is on a map of England. I just tried to upload a map on my iPhone, but the service isn't good enough. So, an hour and a half train ride to Crewe will be followed by a train change, and subsequent train ride to Chester. We should be in Chester by 3:00pm, on the opposite end of England from where we started in London.

I'm bag-less. My backpack didn't arrive on the luggage carousel at Heathrow Airport. Leslie's backpack popped right out, but mine apparently never left Atlanta last night. Our option was to spend the day and night in London, and pick up my bag at the airport tomorrow morning, or just go on with our plan and head to Chester bag-less and have a courier service deliver it later tomorrow for an obscene fee of 150 pounds! Not kidding. But spending a night in London and taking trains back and forth to the airport in the morning would've cost more and we'd probably forfeit what we paid for our hotel in Chester tonight. So, we're on the train to Crewe. Bag-less and on our way to the border of England and Wales.

I had added a second night in Chester (tomorrow) just in case we had a glitch in our flights. So, having my bag show up tomorrow will be fine . . . as long as it arrives tomorrow.

Leslie had a brush with the rich and famous last night! We flew on standby reservations. Free tickets compliments of Seth's pilot parent perks. We missed our first flight at 5:25pm by one seat! We were eighth and ninth on the standby waiting list, and they had eight available seats (not nine). So, we got placed on the standby list for the 8:30pm flight. On that flight, we were the only two on the list, so when we boarded, Leslie got the last first class seat, and I got an aisle seat with the rest of the seats in my row unoccupied. We were both super excited, and had a couple of minutes to talk about the wine list, dinner options, and fully reclining seat-to-bed that Leslie would have. All part of life in seat 8-A. A few minutes after I found my seat, 23-F, I got a text and photo from Leslie of the glass of champagne she was enjoying with her first-class comrades.

No sooner had I called Seth to thank him for our fantastic free tickets and tell him about Leslie's plush digs than I looked up and saw Leslie standing next to me with her champagne flute in hand. Apparently the final first-class passenger arrived right before the doors closed, and Leslie got kicked out of her seat! She did get to sit next to me for seven and a half hours, which I'd like to believe was even better than sitting in first class. But Leslie seemed pretty disappointed.

At least we made the flight and were on our way to London.

Neither of us slept much. A 9:00am arrival at Heathrow was 4:00am Indiana time. But we dealt with arranging my luggage courier, got through the immigration line, then took the Heathrow Express to Paddington Station in downtown London, all seamlessly. The memories of being here two years ago came flooding back. It was around the first of April in 2015 that we flew to London and took the same Heathrow Express to Paddington Station on our way to Minehead, on the west coast of England, to start our 630-mile hike of the West Coast Path.

Paddington Station, and Euston Station for that matter, are super organized chaos. People going every which way. Fifteen or twenty different train platforms with trains coming and going constantly, and all seeming to run like a Swiss watch. When the electronic schedule board says the train will leave at 12:05pm, it leaves at 12:05pm! No jacking around. Uniformed train workers and help desk people are all super helpful, noticing our confused looks and pointing us in the right direction, seemingly without us ever saying a word.

Monday, August 21, 2017 – Chester

A day of waiting around. Since my bag never showed up yesterday, we spent that day, and today, waiting for my dumb backpack. We'd planned to spend this extra day in the town of Chester anyway, so it was a combination of eating, laying around, going for a walk, eating more, laying around some more, doing some local site-seeing, eating again, and then going to bed. This long-distance hiking business is tough.

Chester is old. Apparently, there is a Roman wall here (that we didn't see) that is over 2,000 years old. And a huge, old cathedral (that we walked around) that is pretty cool. Leslie took a photo of me standing next to a 10-foot-tall silver metal pinecone sculpture. We also saw a gigantic pigeon coop, that had 80-100 individual pigeon coop holes. It was around 12 feet by 12 feet. We saw some statues that totally looked like swirled steaming piles of dog turds, and another metal statue that looked like a 60-foot-long missile that got knocked over onto its side. All of these amazing statues were on the grounds of the massive cathedral. So, I'm not sure what that was all about?

The highlights for me were walking the mile and a quarter from our hotel to the start of the Wales Coast Path on the border of England and Wales. I wanted to know how to get to the start before we actually set out tomorrow morning. I did the same thing the day before we started hiking the Southwest Coast Path two years ago. It felt sort of weird standing at the starting line of this 870-mile footpath, and knowing that we'll be hiking on it every day for the next 10-plus weeks!! There was an imprint of a shell, the symbol for this trail, in the sidewalk next to the date "2012." We laid down on the sidewalk next to the shell imprint and took a couple of selfies.

The trail starts alongside the River Dee, and we'll follow the river for the first five miles or so tomorrow morning. We are both excited to start walking and get some miles under our feet!

My second highlight of the day was a big bowl of homemade butternut squash and carrot soup that we had for lunch at a little subterranean lunch spot along the main Eastgate Street. The downtown area of Chester is very cool. Touristy, but full of lots of cool old red brick, stone, and Germanic-looking buildings. Or Austrian-looking. I just read on Google that Chester also has an ancient Roman amphitheater that I initially wanted to go see later this afternoon, but I just looked at some photos of it on the internet and it looked kind of disappointing. So, we'll skip it.

Our plan for the rest of the day (its 3:45pm) is to continue to battle our jet lag and lack of sleep from Saturday night; hopefully get my dumb backpack sometime later today; do a little repacking and reorganizing (I bought a new T-shirt and three pairs of underpants in Chester since I don't have any of my clothes yet); and then find some good dinner and go to bed.

Tuesday, August 22, 2017 – Hiking Day 1
Chester to Flint – 12 miles

We have our first of an estimated 77 hiking days under our belts. It feels really great to be underway and finally walking after all the months of planning and daydreaming.

My backpack finally showed up at the hotel last night at 8:30pm. It cost $200US to have it delivered, but that was really our only option. Considering we flew to England for free (thanks to Seth) it was a small price to pay.

Last night we had dinner at a little street-side café in downtown Chester. It was across the street from a row of old three-story, black-and-white Tudor buildings. Our waiter told us that a few of the original Tudor buildings in Flint are over 400 years old. We had a bottle of Merlot, a yummy brick oven baked pizza, and an arugula salad. Then we picked up some hiking snacks for tomorrow at a grocery store, and were in bed by 9pm. We had reconfirmed at dinner that there is no tipping in the U.K. at restaurants, taxis, bars, barbers, etc.

This morning we were up at 7am. Had another great breakfast at the hotel and had our packs on our backs and walking by 8:17am!! It was a cool, overcast morning. Perfect for hiking. We retraced our 1.1-mile walk to the official start of the Wales Coast Path, just a sidewalk marker on the border of England and Wales. There is the trail symbol, a "dragon-tailed seashell" imprinted into the tarmac, next to a "2012," the year the trail officially opened. And that was it. No big statues or signs marking the start of this 870-mile adventure. We took a few more selfies, and off we walked.

The first part consisted of about 5.5 miles on black pavement along the Dee River. We passed lots of cyclists and several people walking their dogs. We did see one younger lady with a backpack about the same size as ours. We just said hello but I have a feeling we'll see her again over the next few days. It just seemed like she'll be hiking for a while, so we'll find out how far she's going.

The second half of our day was a lot more interesting since we really had to follow the details in our written guidebook and pay attention to the route and the signage. We missed one turnoff and went a couple hundred yards in the wrong direction, but we figured out pretty quickly that we were off-course.

By about mile seven or eight, my legs and ankles were starting to ache. My pack weighs around thirty pounds, Leslie's about twenty-six pounds (we weighed them at the airport). And neither of us has walked (me) or run (Leslie) more than four miles in a day over the past several months of our non-training. We've been telling ourselves that we'll just get in shape while we walk the first couple of weeks, but that doesn't make my legs any less sore.

We took three or four short breaks, but otherwise we hiked the whole 12 ½ miles straight through, past an Airbus airplane factory, past a herd of cows, past some small fishing boats, through an estuary known for its birdlife (we didn't see many), and finishing at Flint Castle, built in 1278!

We walked a few blocks into the town of Flint and had a late lunch at a cute little café run by two older ladies. Their entire menu consisted only of several cold and hot sandwiches. But what we ordered tasted amazing!!

The ladies were happy and smiling, and one said that she "just loved" my accent. She called a taxi for us and we drove the two miles to Mountain Park Hotel, next to a golf course. It was the closest lodging to the trail with vacancy that we could find when I emailed several weeks ago. I pre-made reservations for the first four nights of our hike, since this is considered high tourist season.

After a welcomed shower and nap, we went to the attached bar and restaurant and shared a couple of cold refreshing Strongbow ciders (that were amazing) and a light dinner. Now we're in bed, catching up on emails and work stuff. Leslie is frustratingly trying to figure out her blog site so that she can post some photos from our first day of hiking. Already my legs are feeling better. Our first day done. One day at a time!!

Leslie's Journal Entry:

There is a young woman following us, carrying a big pack. Jon nicknamed her Winifred, and I nicknamed her Gwennie. We don't want to catch her and have to walk together because we are socially awkward freaks.

I forgot my raincoat in Chester—shit!! When to tell Jon?

It started raining. No raincoat.

I had to spill the beans.

Why do I have to blog? Why did I tell people I would? Does anyone care? Do I care? I can't figure the blog site out and am getting really annoyed.

On a positive note, hard cider is my favorite drink.

Wednesday, August 23, 2017 – Hiking Day 2
Flint to Talacre – 13½ miles; Total – 25½ miles

Resting comfortably at our B&B, "The Seascape." Feels a little weird staying in someone's home. Eating in her dining room, using her kitchen, etc. The owner's name is Chriss (yup, with two Ss). She seemed sort of crabby, or maybe just awkward when we met her. Definitely not chatty. She said hello, showed us our bedroom and <u>shared</u> bathroom, told us about the "cold" breakfast options in the morning, and that was the extent of our entire interaction with her.

Leslie was nervous about heating up our dinner and eating down-stairs, but Chriss offered, so we did it. We bought some tasty meat pies and chicken curry pasties at a little bakery in Talacre at the end of our hike and warmed them up for dinner. I also cut up an apple and some cheese that I got from our hotel breakfast two days ago and have been carrying in my pack.

Once we are finished walking for the day, neither of us feel like doing anything other than taking a shower, putting on some clothes that don't stink, and just lying around for the rest of the day and evening. I did a bunch of work on my laptop tonight and read through the details of tomorrow's hike, and then confirmed our Airbnb for tomorrow night. We are only paying $37US for the Airbnb tomorrow, so I'm setting my expectations pretty low.

Today was a good day! Perfect day for hiking. Breezy all day, temps in the low- to mid-60s, and cloudy. The hotel breakfast this morn-ing was $10 each, so instead we caught a taxi at 7:30am and got dropped off at a McDonalds for egg McMuffins and coffee. We picked up some stuff for lunch at a grocery store next to McDonalds, got cash from the ATM, and starting hiking at 8:17am, literally the exact same time we started yesterday.

We went back to the trail, where we left off yesterday at the Flint Castle, and walked the next six or so miles on dirt and gravel trails and grassy paths. Really nice walking along the coast. Nice breeze. We passed the German/Austrian/Swiss lady (not sure which nationality yet) several times during the day. We've given her several names throughout the day including Ingrid, Winifred, and Gwendolyn, and made up several stories about why she's walking alone, how far she's going, etc. One of these days we'll actually ask her name and where she's from. Because everything we know about her so far, we've totally made up.

Around mile seven we passed a huge passenger liner boat that has been out of commission for a decade. Just sitting up on dry land. It was sort of eerie. The trail then led back to the main road connecting Flint to Talacre and followed the sidewalk for the next four and a half miles. We were both getting pretty hungry, so stopped at a little picnic table that was sitting outside of a knitting mill and fabric store tourist stop and had our grocery store lunch. Leslie's chicken salad and corn sandwich looked way better than the buns and cheese that I grabbed at our hotel back in Chester. But I bought a Coke Zero and some chips at the knitting mill to round out my lunch. We were mostly just happy to be sitting down for 45-minutes.

Over the next several miles of road walking, we both got pretty achy and sore. Leslie has a little toe that is rubbing and needed to be coated in Vaseline. And her buttcrack was apparently really chaffing as well!! She didn't do anything about it, or even mention it until it was so badly chaffed that it had started to bleed! This happened to me on our Southwest Coast Path hike two years ago, and it was awfully painful for days. So, I made Leslie stop twice during the ensuing two hours to goop Vaseline into her ass-crack. Apparently the first time she did it, she missed the sorest spot. Because once she lathered her crack a second time, it felt a lot better.

Around mile 11, we walked through a cute little village whose name had like nine syllables and only one vowel, and I think that was a "Y." Then it was back on a grassy track to our end point in Talacre. Talacre is a little beach resort that consists of scores of beach houses and trailers, several ice cream shops, a couple of fish and chips shops, a few little stores selling beach stuff, and, thank God, a pub with a little bakery. So, we stopped to rest our weary bones at about 2:20pm, drank some ale and a berry Strongbow, and feasted on meat-stuffed pasties.

Our B&B was two miles away, so we called a taxi, and for four pounds, were delivered to the front door. It's such a nice feeling to be done hiking for the day. A relief that we don't have to walk again and carry our packs any further, until tomorrow!

Leslie's Journal Entry:

So, we arrived at our B&B, rang the bell, and I swear our hostess was already halfway up the stairs to show us our room upon opening the door, like she could not wait to dispose of us. When we got to the top of the stairs (of course she was already heading back down) she stopped and said, "Oh, can I get you a drink?" Well, if Jon's little eyes didn't just light up like a Christmas tree!

Jon very enthusiastically replied, "Well, sure! What have you got?" She said, "Would you like tea or coffee?" And Jon had to keep up his enthusiasm as to not appear like a drunk, so he said, "Wow! Thanks! Coffee would be awesome," (all while dealing with intense disappointment on the inside).

Personally, I am just happy to be in a cozy room where I can work away until dawn, trying to figure out the stupid blog site!

Three reflections on today's walk:

1. Did I sit on nettle plant, or accidentally take a handful of them and shove them up my ass, because that is how it feels.

2. Blisters are fun to hike 13 and a half miles with, said nobody ever. (Not even Jesus, who did a lot of walking.)

3. Let's see—what sandwich should I have for lunch over the next 75 straight days? Cheese? Cheese and tomato? Cheese and ham? Or tuna mayo?

4. Today Jon said that instead of "A, E, I, O, U, and sometimes Y," like we have in the U.S. alphabet, Wales just has "Sometimes Y." I thought that was funny.

Thursday, August 24, 2017 – Hiking Day 3
Talacre to Abergele – 13¾ miles; Total – 39¼ miles

A "promenade walking day." Most of today's 13¾ miles was on asphalt and pavement. Not great for our feet and my hips. Both of us had sore and tender feet by the end of the day. But there was lots to see, and lots of people watching, which helped the walking tier pass more quickly. The first two to three miles was a nice path between sand dunes. The tall grasses made the path really nice to talk on. There was a breeze blowing into our faces the entire day, and the temperature never got above the low 60s. Leslie has been hiking in a super lightweight windbreaker over a T-shirt. I just wore my T-shirt. As long as we kept moving, I was fine.

The first few miles through the dunes were quiet and peaceful. No people. No sign of Ingrid. Then we walked about a mile on pavement through a huge caravan park full of identical trailers. Actually, I got that backwards—trailer park and then sand dunes. As we neared Prestatyn, we got onto a wide, paved seaside promenade that pretty much went for the next 10 miles through Prestatyn and Rhyl and then eventually into Pensarne and Abergele. We passed a couple of golf courses, two amusement parks, and several places to buy snacks. We stopped at one for some coffee and a scone. We talked about taking more rest stops than we have the first two days. We've been done walking by 2:00 or 2:30pm every day so we have plenty of time on these flat trail days to take more breaks and arrive later in the day.

We stopped for lunch in Rhyl. Another cute seaside resort town. By noon there were lots of people out and about, shopping and walking. Lots and lots of dog walkers and cute dogs to stop and pet. They all made us miss Goldie! We actually walked into Rhyl looking for a camping store to buy Leslie a replacement raincoat. But the one sporting goods store was more of a running store, so no raincoats.

We had a good lunch. It was like two lunches for 8£. I had some kind of spicy noodles with veggies and chicken, and Leslie had chili con carne, which I thought was funny for some reason. I don't imagine her as a chili con carne person. I went up to order at the bar and when I was done I swung around without looking and smashed square into a lady, knocking her backwards. I had to reach out and grab her by the shoulders before she hit the ground. The next time I passed her at the bar a few minutes later, she stepped away to avoid me (with a smile on her face).

Towards the end of the day, when I thought we only had maybe a half-mile to go, I plugged our Airbnb address into my phone and realized we still had three miles to go! Uggh. Leslie said, "Let's just pretend we are starting our day now, and only have three miles to walk today." (As she limped along with her very sore left little toe.)

Our Airbnb was three-quarters of a mile into town, so we walked instead of getting a taxi. The house was a tiny two-floor flat with three bedrooms, a tiny kitchen, and one shared bathroom. Olga emailed us that the place was fully rented out. From what I could tell, two young single guys rented the other two bedrooms. Olga wrote that they worked night shifts at the local hospital. I only saw one of the guys coming out of the bathroom wrapped in a towel. The place was clean, super basic, but good enough for sleeping, and it only cost $35US for the night.

We had to walk another half-mile or so to the main street of Abergele, where most of the restaurants and stores were. It was a cute bustling little town. There are the remnants and ramparts of a huge ancient castle on the hillside just out of town. Nice dinner and a pint (Leslie is sticking with cider). I tried a Doonbar ale.

The next table over had the nicest older local couple in their 70s. The lady works in a hospice center and the man was a retired builder. They were from Abergele and told us a bit about the area. Encouraging us to visit several places that we'll never see because they are all a few miles or more off the trail.

After they left, I noticed an older lady sitting a couple tables away who eventually scooted over to the table next to ours while mumbling something like, "Stupid people here seat a single old lady at a table for four. I don't understand it." Leslie thought it was her excuse for sliding over to strike up a conversation.

Margaret, who turned out to be 91 years old, was super interesting!! She was a little hard to understand with her Welsh accent, and she spoke just above a whisper. She lives in the village and has spent her life as a "UFO-logist." She said, "A lot of people think I'm kind of loony." But she has written two books about UFO encounters, *Who Are They?* and *Link to the Stars* by Margaret-Ellen Fry. We talked quite a while about UFOs and her early years growing up with a father who was a British spy catcher. She was born in Punjab, India, and grew up traveling everywhere. At 91 years old, Margaret wishes her body would let her keep traveling.

She told us about her dozen grandchildren and two dozen great-grandchildren, and said that none of them like to do adventurous traveling and none share her passion for UFOs. I looked up her books on Amazon. They exist but are out of print. I'll try to track down copies of both. Margaret said that she still occasionally gets books sent to her in the mail requesting her autograph.

Margaret seemed lonely and said she doesn't usually come to the pub to eat. It is just something to do to get her out of the house. At 91 years old she still has an amazing and contagious spirit of adventure! I want that to be me if I live that long.

We picked up some yogurt, milk, and breakfast bars for tomorrow's breakfast, plus some more Vaseline (essential), lip balm, butt wipes, and hand sanitizer, and then walked back to our simple little room and its not-very-comfortable bed.

Leslie's Journal Entry:

Reflections on today's walk:

1. Owwwwwwww.

2. It is not that fun to stay in low-income housing after walking almost 14 miles with blisters.

3. What is with this "brown sauce" in all the pubs? What is it? Where does it come from? Where is the BBQ sauce?

Friday, August 25, 2017 - Hiking Day 4
Abergele to Llandudno - 12¾ miles; Total – 52 miles

Up at 7am again. Leslie wasn't feeling too motivated this morning. Her feet are killing her, and she has a couple of blisters on her left foot that are really giving her problems. She has this huge painful blister under her left little toe. I remember her getting a blister in the same place on our last long-distance hike on the Southwest Coast Path. She ended up limping the entire day today and was in noticeable pain. After about a half-mile this morning she said, "This is going to be a long day." She tried two or three different combinations of taping up her toes and feet, but nothing seemed to help other than the eight Advil she took, spaced throughout the day. So, we were a little slower than usual, and took a few extra breaks. But despite it all, we still made it to Llandudno by 2:30pm.

We ate breakfast in our room. I made some instant coffee in the tiny shared kitchen and we had our yogurt and breakfast bars. The first eight or nine miles were all on paved bike trails and sidewalks, which really compounded Leslie's aching feet. After about two hours we stopped in a little seaside restaurant, owned by a famous Welsh chef in Colwyn Bay, and had the best cups of coffee and amazing walnut coffee cake! It was an awesome treat and a really nice break.

There was an older couple sitting at the table next to us, Gareth and Monica Jones, who we ended up striking up a conversation with. We decided to sit and chat for a while. They live on the Isle of Anglesey, where we'll be in a few days. They speak fluent Welsh amongst themselves and Gareth helped me with my mispronunciations of some of the towns we've walked through already. Early on in the conversation he told us that they live in the town with the longest name in the world!! Here it is . . . "Llanfairpwllgwyngyllgogerychchwyrndrobwllllantysiliogogogoch." No shit. You should have heard him pronounce it!!

They gave us their phone numbers and address and invited us to stop over or call if we need anything during our 12-day hike around the Isle of Anglesey.

The rest of the day we walked through Rhos on the Sea, Penrhyn

Bay, and then up and over the "Little Orme," a beautiful rocky outcropping that gave us our first real uphill hiking and about two miles of grassy, dirt trails. Our spirits instantly lifted once we started walking on a real trail. The last three miles or so were back on sidewalks and seaside promenades. Leslie really started to limp and was ready to be done for the day!! Llandudno is an old resort community with dozens of little three-story hotels in old buildings constructed in the 1800s. All lined up along a sandy, crescent-shaped lagoon. All of the hotels are completely packed since today is Friday and the start of a three-day holiday weekend in Wales. We stopped for lunch at a great pub/restaurant, Dillan's, about a quarter mile before we got to the hotel. I had an amazing chorizo and calamari pizza, and Leslie had seabass tacos, and of course some ale. So nice to sit and eat.

We were just talking about how doing a long-distance adventure like this really amplifies how much we appreciate simple things like eating, resting, decent weather, water, feet that don't hurt, a cozy bed. Other things don't seem to matter. It is nice to get rid of the rest of the clutter for a while.

We're staying at the Queen's Hotel, right across the street from the promenade and the ocean. We were originally given a room in the hotel's annex that didn't have an internet connection, so I asked to be moved to another room in the main hotel. We'd already unpacked and taken showers, but I really needed internet so I could get some work done. So, we packed up and moved across the street only to find out that although the main hotel had internet, it was only on the main floor and didn't extend to the hotel rooms. Grrr.

So, I've spent the last two hours in the hotel pub on the main floor getting some work done, responding to emails, and trying to figure out lodging for the next several days. For our first few days on the Isle of Anglesey, there are very few places to stay, and none are along the hiking route and ALL of the few available options are cottages that can only be rented by the week. So, I need to do some more work on getting lodging for the next few days.

It's 9pm and Leslie just hobbled down to join me for a pint of cider and some crisps. A perfect end to the day. So far, we've hiked 52 miles. I'll celebrate that. Cheers!!

Leslie's Journal Entry:

Reflections:

1. We have met such nice people along the way, but I have already forgotten them because all I can think about is how bad my feet hurt!

2. We landed in the well-populated and busy Llandudno and the internet sucks. Bummer. Can't work on the stupid blog.

3. I literally just saw the fattest human baby ever sucking on a bottle of Kool-Aid.

Saturday, August 26, 2017 – Hiking Day 5
Llandudno to Conwyn ~ 9 miles; Total 61 miles

It's getting too late to write. It must be past 9pm!! We are spending our second night at the Queen's Hotel in Llandudno. A couple of days ago, I tried to book any kind of lodging in Conwyn, where we hiked today, but there was nothing available on this busy three-day holiday weekend. Nothing was available. We were able to get a second night here, so we left our backpacks in our room and hiked nine miles today with just a light day pack. It was awesome!

And given the state of disrepair of Leslie's feet, she walked in her Teva sandals all day. Which was also awesome. She's planning on doing the same thing tomorrow to allow her blisters to heal a bit.

I was up early and got take-out coffee and breakfast at a Starbucks. We ate in our room and then started walking about 8:30am. It was a beautiful, cool, partly cloudy morning. We walked to the end of Llandudno and then followed a narrow one-way road all the way around the Grand Orme—a massive rocky hill/mountain that sticks out into the ocean. It was about five miles to get all the way around it. The first half was uphill, and then second half back down. There were virtually no cars, but several Saturday morning bikers and walkers.

We walked along a beautiful sandy beach and the Conwyn Estuary and eventually over a bridge into the old medieval village of Conwyn. There is a huge castle right at the entrance to the town that was built in 1281AD. Almost totally intact. The village is still partly surrounded by castle walls and the entire village retains a Medieval flair.

We got there about 12:30pm and went straight to the George and Dragon Pub for lunch. I had bangers and mash, so good!!! Leslie had a grilled cheese and tomato sandwich (lame). There was a Premier League soccer game on and everyone in the pub was rooting for Manchester City. The match was tied 1-1 when we left. We got a nice lightweight replacement raincoat for the one Leslie accidentally left in Chester at the start of our hike, and I bought a super lightweight hiking T-shirt.

After waiting 20 minutes for a taxi at the city-center taxi stand, we gave up and caught a local bus back to within two blocks of our hotel. Leslie bought some sturdy hiking sandals to try out tomorrow, and we were back taking a short nap in our hotel room by 4:30pm.

Not a hard day. But we got our nine-mile section completed with minimal or no damage to Leslie's already damaged feet. We plan to have a similar low impact day tomorrow as well.

We had a really great dinner of gourmet hors d'oeuvres at a place a few blocks away. I have several work things I need to do, but like I started out writing, I'm pooped. So, it'll have to wait until tomorrow. We've been so lucky with our fifth straight hiking day of good weather. Not a drop of rain while we've been hiking. We'll see how long it holds. One day at a time. And we had fun today and accomplished our hiking goal!!

Leslie's Journal Entry:

Today I walked without a pack and in my flip-flops in the sun! Can you say, "Long-distance hiker orgasm?"

We ate in a small pub today for lunch and Boy George was there watching soccer. I swear it! Isn't he gay? This Boy George look-a-like had a wife.

Sunday, August 27, 2017 - Hiking Day 6
Conwyn to Llanfairfechan - 10 miles; Total – 71 miles

We decided to sleep in a bit today. With only a flat nine or 10 miles to hike, again with a small day pack, there was no need to rush out. Despite my intentions to keep sleeping, I was antsy and wide awake, and heading down to the hotel lobby with my laptop to get some work done by 7am. Starbucks doesn't open until 8am on Sundays, so the guy at the hotel night desk got me a watered-down teacup of coffee from somewhere. I caught up on several disgusting Trump headlines, all of which made me feel disdain for the United States and ever more hatred towards this fuck-knuckle of a president. Most days I'm happy that I'm not allowing myself to be barraged by headlines about this egomaniac.

I got some Hydaburg work done and met Leslie at 8:15am in the hotel dining room for our first "Full Welsh" breakfast. It seems like we had a "Full English" breakfast just about every single day at the

B&Bs and hotels we stayed in along the Southwest Coast Path.

We sat at our assigned table and a waiter with a foreign accent took our order. We both got the Full Welsh breakfast, of course, which was not surprisingly about identical to the Full English we'd had dozens of times during our Southwest Coast Path hike. The Full Welsh included eggs made to order, half of a roasted tomato, a thick slice of what the English and Welsh call bacon—but what we'd call salty ham—a sausage, a slab of black pudding (which I think is the same as blood pudding, and is made out of clotted blood and fried, which I shouldn't have described to Leslie just before we started eating), a half-slice of deep-fried toast (sort of weird, but tasty), regular toast, coffee, and juice. Oh, and a large scoop of baked beans.

We caught a taxi to the Conway Quay (pronounced "key") where we left off yesterday and started on our nine-mile day hike (light day packs) to Llanfairfechan, which is getting more and more fun to say every time I say it. We were treated to some great views of the huge Conway Castle as we walked around the harbor. The first half of the hike was along a dirt trail and through sand dunes. The tide has been out this time of the morning, so sandy beach stretched out for a half-mile in some places. Some folks were already out with their dogs and small children, even though it was only around nine on a Sunday morning.

The second half of the hike ran alongside A-55, a busy highway. So that wasn't as nice, but the scenery both out across the water and inland towards Conway Mountain was beautiful. Leslie hiked in her new hiking sandals for a second day and her feet were fine. I didn't take any Advil today for some reason, and so my legs and hips and back felt achy for most of the day.

We took a short break underneath a train bridge, and I decided to lay down for a few minutes until I got a strong smell of someone else's pee. We took another break along the seashore promenade in a cute little town called Penmaenmawp. We stopped for coffee and a brownie, but mostly just so we could sit in chairs and rest for a while. The little seaside café was selling used books as a fund raiser for the Salvation Army. I'm almost done with my book, *The Poison Artist*, so I bought another book, something by D.H. Lawrence.

Our hike today ended in Llanfairfechen, which I found out was pronounced, "Glanvairvecken." We had a late lunch at a pub. Actually, we only had pints of cider, and then caught a #5 bus back to Llandudno. We got off at a shopping plaza and went to Sports Direct where Leslie bought some new hiking shoe cross-trainers that, when she tried them on, said pinched her toes as much as her current, problematic shoes. But her current ones have over 700 miles on them, are ripping in several places, and have cushioned inserts that are no longer cushiony. So at least these new ones will last longer.

Not-very-good paninis for an early dinner. Naptime until 6pm. Then I spent a few hours in the hotel bar doing work. We made a dash to a local mini mart and got some food for breakfast, and then called it a night. Tomorrow we put our full packs back on once again. Neither of us are looking forward to that.

Leslie's Journal Entry:

So, today is the third day we have been based out of Llandudno and hiked from here.

Reflections on our three days here:

1. Due to my blister situation, I got some, what I would call, sturdy ugly Jesus sandals, or super hip athletic sandals. What is happening to me?

2. Jon is convinced I should just hike in crosstrainers. I was tired and not in the mood to shop and allowed myself to be talked into 80-year-old grandpa mall-walking shoes. What is happening to me?

3. The most beautiful and amazing thing happened today while Jon and I were napping in our *Dick Van Dyke* show twin beds. We had been asleep for an hour and a half, which for Jon is already an unheard-of miracle, when he awoke, looked at his phone, and said, (this is the beautiful part), "I don't want to get up yet, I am just checking at the time." What? What is happening here?

Monday, August 28, 2017 – Hiking Day 7
Llanfairfechan through Bangor to Mein Bridge on the Isle of Anglesey – 12½ miles; Total – 83½ miles

It's a "Bank Holiday" today. The end of a three-day weekend. So, a lot of things are closed, including the post office we were planning to mail some things home from. We'll have to wait and do our mailing on Tuesday out of Mein Bridge.

Breakfast in our room was pretty lame. We'd bought some kind of spice cake and a plastic thing of cut up fresh fruit. And I made instant coffee. All of it was less than appetizing. I had my hopes up for Starbucks coffee, but it opened late this morning due to the damn Bank Holiday. Both of us think our packs are getting heavier. We've bought a few things along the way so far: socks, underwear, a shirt for me, two maps of the Isle of Anglesey, and a little food. Plus, Leslie is now carrying her new hiking shoes as she's going another day in her hiking sandals. Today she wore pink running socks in her purple hiking sandals. Which, with her purple sweatshirt and red backpack, made for some great photos throughout the day.

We caught a cab at 8am for Llanfairfechen to start where we'd left off yesterday. At one point during the ride, I looked up and saw the cab's meter already at 35£. Damn! I think it ended up costing around 48£ ($68US). Yikes! Probably should've just taken the bus again for 3.40£ each.

The highlights today were the people we met. Tommy was our cab driver and we finally got to unload some of our frustrations with American politics and Donald Trump. That was sort of cathartic. Tommy talked about his approach to accepting all people, and his view that we are all basically the same. He told us how he appreciates his kids and grandkids so much more since he suffered a heart attack 10 years ago. He said his heart stopped for 10 minutes and that a total stranger saved his life.

And then later in the day, a couple of miles out of Bangor, we met Peter, a 57-year-old guy who was out for a walk on the trail. We were sitting on an old stone wall taking a little water break and Peter strolled up to say hello. At one point, I asked if he had the day off due to it being a Bank Holiday. He replied that he'd suffered a heart attack eight weeks ago and was now out walking twice a day, thankful to be alive. Two men, in one day, who have a new, or renewed lease on their lives because they came so close to death.

The weather was great today. It started out pretty windy with clouds rolling in and out all day. The sun peeked out from time to time, making for some stunning lighting and great photos. We walked mostly on dirt and gravel trails today, so very little road walking for a nice change. We walked along miles of these ancient slate walls made of thousands of weathered vertical pieces of slate that have served as animal fencing for hundreds of years. We are clearly leaving the more touristy northern coast of Wales, which will be a nice change.

Still no rain on our seventh day of hiking. But I can actually hear a little drizzle outside of the Bulkeley Arms Hotel and Pub window as I'm writing tonight.

At mile nine and a half today, we stopped at the Shipyard Pub for lunch. I had an awesome steak pie with peas and mash, and Leslie got a plowman's special which we remembered from our Southwest Coast Path hike. It's like a charcuterie plate of meats, cheeses, olives, chutney, etc. We each had a pint of cider and felt so full and content after our great meal…until we had to hoist our dumb packs onto our backs. I had a hard time pulling Leslie out of her chair to get back on the trail. Neither of us were in the mood to hike the final three miles of the day. That last part of today's trail included a lot of ups and downs, and the cider really made us sleepy.

We eventually walked up over the Mein Bridge onto the Isle of Anglesey, which we'll be hiking around the shores of for the next 12 days!! Crossing the bridge onto Anglesey also marked the completion of the first section of the overall Wales Coast Path, that has seven total sections. So, we've completely gone through our first hiking guidebook. It's one of the things I'll mail home tomorrow when the post pffice opens. It was just another half mile to the Bulkeley Arms that had an amazing modern room above this 150-year-old pub. Fancy bathroom. Awesome comforter on the bed. Really nice room.

I spent a couple of hours in the pub doing work and then we went to a Bangladeshi restaurant for out-of-this-world butter chicken curry! Tomorrow we head out along the shore of the north part of Anglesey to a B&B in the countryside, about 10 miles away.

Leslie's Journal Entry:

OMG. I just had the best butter chicken ever!

There is a reason there is an Indian restaurant on every block in the U.K.—butter chicken!

SECTION TWO:
ISLE OF ANGLESEY

Tuesday, August 29, 2017 – Hiking Day 8
Mein Bridge to B&B near Penmon
10 miles; Total – 93½ miles

Leslie just Googled "bloody butt chaffing." No need to go into further detail. Suffice to say that it was a mistake to click on "images." Anyway, my medical wisdom has once again been confirmed. It said to completely dry out the ass-crack and then use talcum powder. And then use petroleum lubricant (read—Vaseline) when physically active. That's what I've been saying for the past few days!

I just asked Leslie what the highlights of the day were, and she replied, "Lunch, but not dinner." So, I'll start there. We bought lunch and dinner from a small grocery store in Beavmaris this morning at about 11:30am as we passed through town, knowing that there would be no more stores or restaurants for the rest of our hike today, or anywhere near our B&B tonight.

So, for lunch I got a curry chicken salad sandwich and sea salt and vinegar potato chips, and Leslie got a chicken salad sandwich with the same kind of chips. And we topped lunch off with several Oreo cookies. For dinner, which we just ate here at the B&B, we got two oranges, four cold meat pasties, and more Oreos. We also made a pot of tea. We had to buy lunch for tomorrow, too, since we won't pass anything for the initial nine or 10 miles or our hike.

The B&B is outside of Penmon, a tiny village, and is owned by Phil and his wife or partner? Not sure about that. She looks a lot older than Phil so who knows? We are in a bedroom with an attached breakfast room that is connected to the main house. We have our own bathroom, too. It's actually a really nice place. We got here around 3pm and have just been lazing around. Showers, naps, and then office work, reading, and catching up on emails and news.

Most of our hike today was either on trails crossing through cow and sheep pastures or walking along the beach. So, it was really nice hiking with beautiful scenery! The village of Beavmaris was really cute. There is an old 12th century castle there. We also passed the remnants of an abbey that was built in the 11th century! Really unbelievable!! We saw a little lighthouse at Penmon Point and shared some coffee there. We had our lunch sitting on an old sea wall facing the water, looking out towards Puffin Island. The few buildings and stone walls around where we ate all looked super old, built hundreds of years before the U.S. was even a country.

Today felt like we were finally getting away from the tourists and road walking, and out into the Welsh countryside. Not many or any opportunities to stop to buy snacks or eat lunch in a restaurant or seaside café, but the hiking and views and peacefulness are a lot more rewarding and enjoyable.

Still no rain while hiking. Every day we are ready for it. It drizzled through most of the night last night but had stopped by the time we started walking this morning at 9:20am. We didn't get our Welsh breakfast until 8:30am, and then I mailed some things home at the post office, which didn't open until 9am. Time to finish my murder mystery and then get some sleep. Big hiking day tomorrow.

Leslie's Journal Entry:

Wednesday, August 30, 2017 – Hiking Day 9
Phil's B&B near Penmon to Moelfre
14 miles; Total – 107½ miles

We hit our 100-mile mark today!! Just before we reached Pentra-eth Beach. From the time we walked out of Phil's front door to our 10½ mile mark in Benllech, we didn't pass by any commercial buildings. It was all farmer's fields, old dirt farm roads, and walking on bluffs above the ocean, with some nice beach walking around Red Warf Bay mixed in. It was really enjoyable for the most part. To the extent that walking these initial 10-plus miles with a backpack can be called fun, it was fun. Lots to look at. Just incredible scenery. And again, the sun and clouds danced together all day long, making for some great photos.

Phil provided his "vegetarian" breakfast at 8:30am in the little breakfast room next to our bedroom. He served cold cereal and coffee, and then made eggs and toast. He also brought us four fresh plums from their tree that were super sweet. We carried with us today our lunch that we'd bought yesterday morning. Two remaining meat pasties from last night's dinner, and some chicken, cheese, and bread left over from yesterday's lunch.

At around the eight-mile point of the day, we decided to celebrate hitting our 100-mile mark while sitting at a picnic table. I took a picture of a pepperoni stick next to two coins, to represent "100." With 770 miles to go, it's not a major milestone to hit 100 miles, but it was a bit of a psychological boost.

At around nine miles, we passed a pub called The Ship's Inn. There were a few dozen picnic tables outside and a sign in front that said people couldn't sit at the picnic tables unless they bought food at the inn. So, I went inside and bought two Pepsi soft drinks and some chips, and we sat at a picnic table that was the furthest away from the inn.

When Leslie opened her pack to get our lunch stuff out, she realized that her full water bottle had totally emptied itself inside her pack. Most everything we are carrying is stored in waterproof stuff sacks, so only a few things were sitting in a small pool of water at the bottom of her pack.

Right as we were finishing our lunch, a Ship's Inn server came over to tell us that this wasn't a picnic area, and that we needed to stop eating our own food. I explained that we'd actually bought chips and drinks in the pub and brought them out, but she wasn't persuaded. She pointed out the "no picnicking" signs posted along the drive into the parking area. I told her that we'd walked in on the beach from the opposite direction. She didn't care. I thanked her for telling us and since we were basically done eating anyway, we packed up and left. No special exceptions for backpackers who'd just hit their 100-mile mark.

Another two miles took us to the cute little seaside village of Benllech, virtually all of which we passed through while on a beautiful sandy beach because the tide was out. In Benllech we walked about a half-mile uphill and away from the sea to our B&B for the night, run by Dee and Martin. Martin met us at the door, and we dropped our packs in our nice room. We grabbed the trail guide and some money and headed right back out the door to walk our final three miles to Moelfre, another very cute little village that didn't have any lodging.

Even with the last three miles being pack-less, 14 miles is still a long way to walk, especially since it included a fair bit of ups and downs. We'd been excited to get dinner in Moelfre, and Martin had offered to come pick us up afterwards. But we found out that the two places that serve food didn't start serving until after 6pm. Since it was only a bit after 4pm when we got there, we settled in for a pint of ale while sitting at a picnic table and looking out at the water while we enjoyed the ale.

We asked the pub to call a taxi for us, and we went back to Benllech to instead have a nice dinner at The Benllech. I had my first fish and chips in Wales, and Leslie had an Indian dish. The pub bartender turned us on to a rum and ginger beer drink that hit the spot. We each had a couple of those and walked back to our B&B for showers and the rest of the night. Every other night or so we look ahead to where we are going and try to book lodging somewhere that won't be too far from the trail. So, I made some bookings tonight for September 2nd and 3rd.

Leslie's Journal Entry:

Thursday, August 31, 2017 – Hiking Day 10
Moelfre to Amlwch
12 miles; Total – 119½ miles

We just finished the most beautiful stretch that we've hiked so far. It just kept getting more and more pretty and dramatic the further we walked. It also felt more and more like we were on the Southwest Coast Path of England. Lots of climbing up and down hills and ridges and knobs. Lots more stair steps to grunt up. We had a "picnic" lunch around mile eight and a half, high up on a soft grassy spot that overlooked the sea. The last couple of miles got kind of long. We'd convinced ourselves that we were close to Amlwch but ended up walking and walking for another hour and a half.

The sky got really dark and rained hard at around 10:30am. The rain almost felt like hail. We quickly put on our raincoats and pack covers for the first time on this trip. It was a cold, biting rain, but only lasted 15 minutes or so. It took us too long to get our rain stuff on, so next time we'll be quicker and more ready. I was already pretty soaked by the time I dug out my raincoat. Our experience in the chilling rain made us think that we need to buy fleece hats pretty soon. If it had been rainy and windy all day, we would have been freezing.

A highlight of the day was meeting two different couples. The first couple was hiking the Wales Coast Path in day-long sections. They take two to three weeks off every year to hike several day sections of the trail, meaning they only carry a light day pack every day. This year they are hiking the Isle of Anglesey section. They were from somewhere near Liverpool and are camping in a trailer at Church Bay, where we'll be in a couple of days. They said that a lot of people hike around the Isle of Anglesey the other way around, clockwise. Our guidebook has us going counterclockwise.

We have seen two people for sure so far who had larger packs, hiking the opposite direction that we were going. One guy was wearing big, heavy leather hiking boots and was limping as we passed him walking through Mein Bridge. Other than the two we met today, we haven't seen or met anyone going our direction who looks like the are on a multi-day hike.

The second couple was day hiking and we met a few miles before we got to Amlwch. They were from somewhere in England as well and own a "Holiday House" trailer nearby that they stay in several times a year. They told us a bit about the area and talked about how beautiful this part of Wales is. They then pointed us in the right direction, since we met them at a trail intersection and I wasn't sure which way to go.

Tonight, we're staying at the Tree Castell Inn that is located right on the water, and right on the trail. It was about two miles past the end of our hike today, so we took a taxi there after finishing our hike to Amlwch Port. We'll take a taxi back tomorrow morning when we're ready to start again.

Leslie was saying today as we were walking that if she was writing a journal, her entries would be something like, "Day 5 – had ice cream;" and "Day 8 – My feet are killing me, and I have my ass chaffing under control."

Leslie's Journal Entry:

Friday, September 1, 2017 – Shauna's Birthday
Hiking Day 11, Amlwch to Cemaes
8 miles; Total – 127½ miles

So, we arrived at the Tree Castell Inn, consisting of a pub with a nice dining area, and several rooms upstairs. We walked up to the desk and a pleasant, round chap with the face of a little boy comes into the office, all red-faced and says in a high-pitched voice, "Sorry, I've been carrying a load of towels up and down the stairs and am a bit winded." All face-flushed and sweaty. He immediately reminded me of a "lollypop kid" on the *Wizard of Oz*. He said, "Where are you from anyway?" "Indiana," we replied. "Lovely," he said, then continued, "I've never been to the U.S. Would love to go. Of course, Indiana would be the first place I'd go. And then to New York. Just to say I've been to New York. But Indiana for sure." And then he smiled, and flushed, and sweated some more. WTF?

We both started giggling as soon as we walked away with the room key. Indiana isn't the first place anyone would go on their first trip to the U.S. . . . ever.

When we left the Trecastell (pronounced "tray caseggh," with the "ggh" sounding like you're trying to clear your throat). The owner, who describes himself as grumpy on the sign out on the street, said to watch for seals and dolphins as we walk along the trail. We hadn't been walking 10 minutes when Leslie pointed to a little black bobbing thing just off the rocks that I proudly announced was a little black seal head peeking out of the water to watch us walk past.

So, we stared at each other for a while, and he never moved and never dove, and I finally realized it was just some black thing floating in the water. Then, a few minutes later Leslie pointed out a round yellowish thing in the water and asked, "What is that?" I took a good look and proudly announced that it was a little otter lying on his back. Probably cracking open a clam shell or eating an abalone. You could see his little black feet sticking out of the water about two feet away from his fuzzy little head. "Why is his face yellow?" Leslie asked. "It's just his little whiskered face pointing up towards the sun. See his little feet sticking up on the other end? They love to lay on their backs. I don't see him eating anything, but he's probably just resting." Leslie yelled down to the little guy to try and startle him.

Around the next corner, we saw another little face sticking out of the water with little black toes poking up two feet away, and then a little orange head. After seeing the second orange-headed otter, Leslie started laughing her head off at me for being so sure that I'd seen two sea otters instead of the two buoys that they actually were. We eventually saw a guy in a small fishing boat going from buoy to buoy checking the crab pots or whatever they were marking. Leslie reminded me that he must be checking the otters.

Our hike was only eight miles today. We caught a taxi to where we stopped yesterday at the Amlych Port and walked the first two miles to a co-op grocery store for snacks, and then back to our hotel where we picked up our packs to go the next six miles to Cemaes. Our guidebook and the hotel owner told us this was the hilliest section of the Isle of Anglesey portion of the Wales Coast Path, with a gain of something like 2,500 feet. Today's hike included the highest point of the trail on the island, as well as the farthest northern point of Wales.

The scenery was once again stunning, with much higher sheer rock cliffs along a jagged, rocky coast. There were three significant drops to sea level and then back up several hundred feet to the next ridge. Purple heather, spikey gorse bushes, an almost cloud-free sky, and a nice cool breeze. Really a beautiful day. On the steep stairstep uphills, Leslie just puts her head down and powers straight up them, non-stop, no matter how high or how many steps.

We passed an old abandoned brick works from the 1800s. And another derelict stone mansion also from the 1800s, and then finally a small cemetery and stone church. The church was initially constructed in the 6th century!

On into little Cemaes, a cute little fishing village. We're staying at the Woburn Hill Hotel. We're sitting in the little hotel bar having beer and wine before dinner. It was nice to have a relatively short day today. Only eight miles that took just under four hours of walking, with some great leg and butt exercise thrown in.

Leslie's Journal Entry:

Saturday, September 2, 2017, Hiking Day 12
Cemaes to Church Bay (Slept at Ferry Lodge in Holy Head)
12½ miles; Total – 140 miles

Boston Arms Pub and Rooms. Remember that name! After our 11-mile, fairly difficult hike from Cemaes to Church Bay, I poked my head into a little beachside café, the first of any kind of establishment we'd seen all day. I bought a couple of Diet Cokes and asked if they could call us out a taxi from Holy Head, another 12 miles away. There was no lodging in or anywhere near Church Bay, so Leslie had reserved a room at the Boston Arms, a pub with rooms that was situated literally right on the trail as it enters the outskirts of Holy Head. We actually reserved it for two nights, since tomorrow we'll get a ride back to Church Bay and hike the 13 miles from there back into Holy Head.

The taxi lady dropped us off in front of a normal-looking pub on very busy road. The Boston Arms. We walked into the pub and there were eight or 10 people at the bar, all yelling and singing at the top of their lungs to whatever music was playing. They all seemed completely shit-faced at 3pm on a Saturday. I had to yell to be heard by the bartender, telling him that we had a room booked. So, a bleach-blonde, had-to-be a prostitute, with tons of make-up and who also seemed drunk, led us to Room #3, located direct-ly above the bar. Actually, all three rooms they had were above the bar.

We got inside and closed the door, and the floor and walls were just shaking from the music. And we could hear everyone yelling and singing, loud and clear. We were both like, "Oh my God. We can-not stay here for two nights." We were originally considering three nights in Holy Head, since on Monday (the day after tomorrow), we can do the next 12 miles with a day pack again; the trail loops around and ends up only a few miles from where it starts.

I immediately got on the internet and we found a nearby hotel and booked it for the next two nights. I went down to pay. The guy asked if I was paying for both nights and I told him we'd just pay for one night at a time and gave him 55£.

Back upstairs, Leslie had finished her shower and was lying in bed trying to nap. We were both exhausted, but Leslie especially. She said she woke up tired and had felt exhausted and low energy all day. We both sat there, walls literally shaking, floor trembling, and just laughed at first. We figured we just had to deal with it for one night. The music and the singing and the yelling were so loud; it was sort of funny because the whole situation seemed so crazy.

I walked to a store next door, and bought some shampoo, butt wipes, and two cans of pre-mixed gin and tonic drinks. What a brilliant idea that is! We sat on the bed and popped open the first gin and tonics, and were like, "This is fucking crazy." A couple of times Leslie seemed like she was going to cry. I asked her twice if she was crying. She said she felt like it.

My turn in the shower. While under the hot streaming water I realized we needed to get the hell out of here. They will be partying with music blaring until 2am! It's a Saturday. We won't get any sleep. We'll be super annoyed and exhausted before we even start our 13-mile hike tomorrow.

I got out of the shower and shook Leslie out of her semi-nap, and said, "We are getting out of here." We both got on the internet and had a horrible time finding a room anywhere in Holy Head. Everything was booked. We checked Orbitz, Trivago, Airbnb, bed and breakfasts, etc. etc. I finally found The Ferry Lodge, only three-quarters of a mile away. I called and they had only one room left, so we begged her to hold it for us, stuffed all of our belongings back in our packs, and literally ran out the side door to the blasting sounds of "wastin' away again in Margaritaville."

We were so happy to be out of that shit hole. Screw the 55£ we'd paid. I could care less. And Leslie was beside herself with joy. She said she's never loved me more than at that moment.

When we checked in at the Ferry Lodge, a little three-story, five-suite B&B, we told the owner lady the whole story. She laughed and said, "The Boston Arms is the worst possible place you could have chosen in Holy Head. Those people weren't drunk at 3pm, they are just crazy. The place is known for having crazy people!!" Oh my God. That explains the bleach-blonde hooker that showed us our room.

It's 8:45pm. We are snug in our room and couldn't be happier.

Oh, our hike today. Suffice to say it was medium difficulty and took us through just about every type of terrain and scenery. Grassy fields, steep and rocky headlands, across a pebble beach, all the way around and right past a huge nuclear power plant just outside of Cemaes, and through prickly gorse bushes. The scenery, once we got past the nuclear power plant, was amazing once again. We passed a cool multi-hundred-year-old lighthouse sitting out on an island, and read about the dozens of catastrophic shipwrecks that have happened off this coast over the last 300 years.

The wind was in our face all day long and it was really sunny. So, by the end of our hike, the sun and wind had taken their toll. Today's section ended in Church Bay, which is really just a little campground, a beautiful sandy beach, a little beachfront café, and a restaurant. We stopped in the café to buy a couple of Diet Cokes and asked if they'd call a taxi for us, which is where today's journal entry started.

They guy behind the café counter was interested in our hike, and the fact that we'd been walking for 12 days. After I paid for our Diet Cokes, and after he'd called a taxi for us, he came out and said he lived in Holy Head and wondered if we needed a ride back out to Church Bay tomorrow morning instead of taking a 30£ taxi ride. A super nice offer. He doesn't leave for work until 9:30am, a bit later than we usually start hiking, but we graciously took Darren up on his offer. So, we'll meet him Sunday morning at 9:30am for the drive back out to Church Bay and the start of our 13-mile walk. It is supposed to rain most of the day tomorrow, so it could be a chilly one.

Leslie's Journal Entry:

Current situation. . . .

We walked 11 miles uphill today. I was feeling lethargic all day and it was tough for me. At one point during the day, I stepped in a warm, creamy, fresh cow pie that oozed into the crevices of my grandpa shoes and into my socks. This did not help my mood.

We finally got to our hotel, which was also a pub. We walked in and everyone, who happened to be totally drunk at 3pm and singing hits from the 80s at the top of their lungs, completely stopped and stared at us.

We were taken to our room, above the bar mind you, where the room was shaking to the beat of "Wake me up before you go go," and we could hear the drunks singing.

Thank God, my amazing husband just asked if we could stay here three nights instead of the two we already booked. (What is he thinking? I want to kill myself right now.)

Then . . . I take off my shoes and socks. OMG!! Cow pie rancid vomitous odor fills the room. Awesome.

No soap or shampoo in our room. Have I said that I want to kill myself right now?

I go to the window to look off in the distance and regroup, when off in the distance I spy a gorgeous "Travel Lodge" sign. Jon calls to see if a room is available for tomorrow.

I love him.

It's full.

We look at each other, and immediately get on our devices, and try to find a place, anyplace, to get out of here, NOW!

We find a place! We are packing up and breaking free of this mistake.

Sunday, September 3, 2017, Hiking Day 13
Church Bay to The Ferry Lodge, Holy Head
14 miles; Total – 154 miles

If you look around our B&B bedroom there is a pair of rain pants and a long sleeve shirt hanging from clothes hangers in the window; an orange daypack, Green Bay Packer ball cap and red raincoat hanging off the wall-mounted TV; two pairs of my shorts and a blue windbreaker hanging over a small closet door; Leslie's black rain pants and blue raincoat hanging off the side of the closet; Leslie's T-shirt and shorts on hangers inside the closet; and two pairs of socks, one pair of underwear, and Leslie's black tights draped over a radiator that isn't turned on. Oh, and two pairs of stinky hiking shoes stuffed with newspaper to absorb some of the water inside them.

That pretty much describes our day today. We started walking at 10am, and it rained, misted, and sprinkled constantly until 2:30pm. And the wind blew a steady 10-15mph all day long. We were both soaked to the bone a couple of hours into the hike. But we got 14 miles in. It was only supposed to be 13, but more about that later.

Since Darren, the Church Bay café guy who offered up a ride back to Church Bay this morning, didn't need to be at work until 10am, we had a slow morning. I was up at 6:30am making coffee and doing some computer work, but Leslie slept in until just before 8am, and so we went down for our B&B breakfast at 8:30am.

We packed our daypacks with food, water, guidebook, map, snacks, and a few other little things like rain pants, and walked to the co-op grocery store to buy lunch and a decent cup of coffee. Once again, we got the "meal deal" of a sandwich, chips, and a drink of your choice for only £3.50. Now that's a meal deal! I got a bacon and chicken sandwich, a bag of Sun Chips, and a large Red Bull.

Darren arrived right at 9:30am as planned and we were back in

Church Bay and on the trail by 10am. Darren is a college student studying sports physiology and health, or something like that. But he wants to be a trainer for a professional rugby or soccer team after he graduates. A super nice guy. And we really appreciated the ride back to Church Bay. It saved us £30.

So, on to the 13-mile hike that ended up being more like 14 miles. We started walking in a light, misty rain. Leslie had her raincoat and rain pants on. I just had my raincoat and Packer hat on, with shorts. Throughout the day, there were several minor ups and downs, but nothing major. The high grassy fields were drenched with rain, so within minutes our feet were soaked. It sort of drizzled and misted for a couple of hours, and then rained hard and blew for another couple of hours. For most of the day we walked, heads down, hoods up, into the wind. Rain running down our faces. The hiking shorts that I was wearing were soaked through quickly, so I never bothered putting on my rain pants. What would be the point?

The trail led along a few beaches. We stopped very briefly to drink some water after two hours, but it was so chilly and windy that neither of us felt like stopping for a break. We just wanted to keep moving.

Just past a sandy beach called Porth Tywyn-mawr, the signed path led through a caravan park. Somehow, I got turned around and we ended up on a small country road going right through the middle of a cluster of farm buildings, barns, sheds, and houses. I guess we were trespassing since we literally walked through the middle of someone's property. We found our way back to the signed path at the next beach, called Proth Penrhyn-mawr (pretty similar to the name of the last one), and the guidebook said, "Follow along the beach for one mile to a house with a slate roof, go another 300 meters and watch for a trail sign heading left."

Well, after only 10 minutes or so, we passed a big lone house with a slate roof, but all of the houses around here have slate roofs. Literally. I knew we hadn't gone anywhere near a mile, so I didn't pay any attention, and we kept on walking along the beach. We walked, and we walked, eventually around a sort of peninsula. I never got out my map; it is made of paper and it was raining. Eventually, we hit a river that was draining an estuary and it was too deep to cross. So, I knew I'd screwed up . . . a second time, since I'd already messed up in the caravan park.

I realized that the big lone slate roofed house we'd passed a half hour before must've been the place to turn inland. So, I decided to just follow the shoreline of the estuary inland because I knew that sooner or later, we'd have to hit the trail. The map (which I eventually pulled out) showed that the trail led about a mile into the estuary to a narrow spot, and then across a small footbridge, then another mile back out to a point that was literally a stone's throw from the spot we were standing, but across the river.

So, we started hiking cross country to intercept the trail. Well, that was probably my third poor decision of the day. We ended up walking through muck and marsh and swampy reeds, all as the rain came down and the wind continued to blow. Just stopping for a minute or two was enough to start one of us shivering. We eventually had to climb over one barbed wire fence, and then a second .

I knew we were getting close to the trail. We had to be, but the weeds and reeds were too tall to see anything and we couldn't see the estuary bridge or anything that looked like a trail. Leslie finally suggested that we leave the muddy estuary bank and just angle inland towards where the trail should be, and that ended up being a very good call. Within 10 minutes we hit the trail. By this time, it was close to 2pm, but still raining, so we just kept on walking. At least we were back on the trail. It stopped raining around 2:30pm and we took a break by a big rock that we could sit on and get off our feet for a little bit.

We were both pretty much soaked to the skin and finally made it back to the Ferry Lodge B&B around 4pm. Exhausted. Aching feet. Chilled. But we were done for the day. We (I) actually made one more wrong turn after we'd stopped for lunch in a subdivision of houses. I think the trail signs were screwed up. But whatever. All-in-all I think we walked at least one extra mile and probably more. Hence our 14-mile day.

After showers, laying around, and warming up a bit, we went to an Indian restaurant down the street for some great butter chicken and naan bread. Definitely the highlight of a long, cold, wet day.

Leslie's Journal Entry:

Wylfa to Abersoch. There is an honor bar out in the unstaffed lobby of our hotel that Jon is calling "the free bar."

Me: *Honor means you on your honor to pay.*

Jon: *But nobody would ever know.*

Did he have no mother?

Monday, September 4, 2017, Hiking Day 14
The Ferry Lodge, Holy Head, around Holy Head Island to Treardoor. 12 miles; Total – 166 miles

Today was completely different from the last 13 days of hiking! We hiked the entire day in a dense fog. It was also really windy all day long. The description in our guidebook for today's hike started out, "This is one of the most dramatic sections of the entire Coastal Path." Back to the thick, pea soup fog. There was a lot of elevation gain today. About 2,000 feet up to just below the top of Holy Head mountain. Several of the 12 miles were rocky and rugged, and the entire day was super windy and blustery. The views of the ocean were supposed to be amazing, but we literally never saw a thing, just what was 100 feet in front of us. It never rained, thank God, or it would have been a much colder hike. But the damp fog and 10-15mph winds kept us moving, and like yesterday we just weren't in the mood to stop for breaks.

We passed several dramatic rock formations, walked right past a big lighthouse and natural stone arch, and never saw a thing. Apparently, there are a lot of well-known rock climbs in the area as well. We actually did see two young guys with packs and a climbing rope heading out . . . in the fog. Crazy.

At about the halfway point in today's mileage, the trail crossed a parking lot with a little café run by some kind of national nature conservancy organization. The fog was still as thick as pea soup. So, we stopped and had some hot coffee and a piece of lemon cake. Leslie said that the favorite part of our hike so far has been getting a piece of cake, which we've done two or three times. The café also had a little gift shop, and I bought Leslie a pair of new, cozy hiking socks since one of her two pairs still smells like the huge cow pie she stepped in the day before yesterday.

Onward. The trail ended up leveling out for the last few miles, and the fog lifted just enough so we could see the ocean that we'd been walking along for most of the day, as well as some sheer cliffs that dropped down to the water. As the weather cleared a bit, we started to see a few day hikers, too. At one point the trail passed some old stone circles that were remnants of stone structures or shelters that were built by Irish raiders around 470AD!!

Our hike ended as we entered the little village of Treardoor. We made good time today, 12 miles in around five hours, but we only took that one break for coffee and cake. When the weather is crappy we just want to keep moving. We asked a lady at a lifeboat station to call a taxi, so we could get back to where we'd started, which even though we hike 12 miles, we walked in a loop and ended up only 3 miles from where we'd started.

Leslie has been feeling crappy this afternoon. Chilled and sort of nauseous. Tired all day. She didn't eat anything for lunch and it's 6:15pm now. She has her warm jacket on in the room. She's also had a pounding headache going on two full days now. She got some migraine meds at a pharmacy when we got back, and took them on an empty stomach. So maybe that's the reason she feels pukey. We decided to go to a decent restaurant tonight instead of pub food or Indian food. It's a few miles away, The Black Seal, so we'll get a taxi and try something different.

Leslie's Journal Entry:

Tuesday, September 5, 2017, Hiking Day 15
Treardoor to Four Mile Bridge and on to Llanfairyneubwll (the Cymyran Hotel). 11miles; Total – 176 miles

Wet and really stinky feet have become a bit of an annoyance for both of us, and an obsession for Leslie. Today we started a competition in the morning to see who could keep their feet the driest while hiking throughout the day. I could cut to the chase and just say that Leslie won, but I won't do that just yet.

For the past couple of days, we've been walking in the rain. By day's end, our shoes and socks are always completely soaked. Several days ago, our shoes really started to stink. Leslie's because she stepped in a huge, soft, custardy cow pie, and me because my shoes just stink for some reason. We bought some kind of medicated foot stink spray that Leslie religiously sprays inside and outside of both of our pairs of shoes at the end of each day.

Well, the wetness really amplifies the stink and for the last couple of nights Leslie has been groaning and protesting about how bad our shoes stink, and how bad our room at the Ferry Lodge stinks as a result. She even sprayed the Glade bathroom air freshener around the room several times to no apparent improvement. We've also stuffed our shoes with newspaper each night to soak up moisture, and that actually really seems to help. The newspaper is always soaking wet by morning.

Anyway, back to the dry shoe competition.

Leslie was wearing the brand new socks she got yesterday and DID NOT want to get them wet. She was already carrying three wet pairs in her pack. So, even though it was misty and raining lightly for the first two hours of our hike, we dodged puddles and walked around low sections of trail and did all manner of hopping and jumping to avoid water. But since it has been raining the last few days, and these rocky headlands with their thin layer of soil just don't seem to be able to absorb all of the water.

My shoes were soaked through pretty much right away, partly because I started the day with socks that were already damp. But Leslie kept her feet pretty dry until we had a trail choice to make around mile seven, where we could either take the road, which was a little longer, or the slightly shorter trail through woods and pastures. I of course picked the shorter route and it ended up being the muddiest, swampiest mile of the entire trip so far. At one point, I even slipped and fell to my knees in the mud. I declared Leslie the winner and we both proceeded to get soaked from there on.

Overall, the walking went well. The rain eventually stopped, and it was actually a decent hiking day. At the nine-mile point, we stopped in a tiny café at "Four-Mile Bridge" a little one-room place run by an elderly lady. We had snacks in our packs, but we decided to stop for a rest and have lunch indoors while sitting at a real table, in real chairs. I had homemade tomato soup and some homemade bread, and we shared some sweet potato fries. Leslie had a ham and cheese toastie.

Which brings me to breakfast. We ended up staying at the Ferry Lodge for three nights. The owner offers a full breakfast for £5 per person, per day, which we paid for upfront when we paid for the room. The first morning, all four rooms were full, so there were several people having breakfast in the little breakfast room. Individual place settings were set at all the tables. Juice and milk pitchers were full and available, and the owner, Sarah, came right out and took our orders. Great breakfast.

The second morning, there was just one other guy staying there besides us. He is from Florida actually. The first person from the U.S. we've met on the trip. He was traveling alone and was sort of negative about everything. No sign of Sarah initially, and the juice pitcher was still sitting partially filled from yesterday. And no milk until the guy asked for some. It seemed like Sarah had just woken up, even though the sign on the dining room door says, "Breakfast sittings at 7:30am and 8:30am," and we were down at 7:45am. Anyway, it was another good breakfast. Just a little disjointed.

This morning . . . morning number three at the Ferry Lodge, we were the only ones staying in the place. No sign of Sarah or any food at 8:15am when we came down for breakfast. I opened up the breakfast room door and turned on the lights. The empty juice pitcher was sitting there on the counter where I'd left it yesterday. We waited about 10 minutes. I knocked loudly on Sarah's apartment door twice, and she never came out. We finally decided that she wasn't even there. The front door wasn't locked, and a bag of garbage that I'd taken out of our room yesterday, and put in the entryway, was still sitting there this morning.

So, I had some stale cold cereal (there was milk in the little fridge) and a yogurt I'd bought at the corner store. Leslie had some instant oatmeal. It wasn't a horrible breakfast, but the fact that we'd already paid and Sarah was nowhere to be found was a little annoying.

Tonight, we are in a nice hotel, the Cymyran, located right next to a Royal Air Force base. Nice bar. Nice restaurant. I taught the bartender how to make a "whiskey sidecar," my favorite whiskey drink. There are very few mixed drinks in this country. And nobody mixes anything with whiskey.

Leslie's Journal Entry:

Jon said he can't wait to get back to our "jail cell." referring to our room. I thought that was funny. You have to suck your stomach in to be able to move around the room.

We ate snacks in bed for dinner, like the grandparents in *Willy Wonka and the Chocolate Factory*.

It rained for six hours straight and our feet and shoes smell like shit. Worse, actually. Nobody said long-distance hiking would be glamorous, but I didn't think cab drivers would roll their windows down when we got in.

Wednesday, September 6, 2017, Hiking Day 16
Llanfairyneubwll (the Cymyran Hotel) to Aberffraw.
13 miles; Total – 189 miles

We just finished having a one-sided conversation for an hour and a half with an Anglican priest who was an enigma wrapped in a riddle, and full-blown full of himself. He is the head priest for the entire island and Anglesey, overseeing something like 55 local parishes. We stopped for the day at a little tea shop/café in Aberffraw. We got here at 2pm and our B&B doesn't open its door until 4pm. So, we were sitting outside talking to a nice couple who told us about a new T.V. show that airs tomorrow night at 9pm called *Safe House*. I noticed that this priest dressed in his black clerical shirt and white clerical collar, just standing off to the side waiting to talk with us.

The priest turned out to be pretty interesting. He initially asked us what we were doing and where we were going, and then he launched into a monologue of the dozens of countries he's visited, and the gang of rough guys he ran with when he was young. He showed us a big tattoo of a naked lady on one forearm, and a griffin or some kind of hideous gargoyle on his other forearm. He told us all about his motorcycle, and a big motorcycle accident he was in. And about how people don't believe he's a priest because of his background, and how nine of twelve of his old buddies have been in prison. And one of his buddies murdered someone. And on, and on, and on.

He was actually funny and entertaining, but it was like he was doing this routine that he does with everyone he's meeting for the first time. He told several stories of how he's helped hikers, or prayed for people during his travels, or comforted strangers, or whatever, in between showing us his tattoos. It got annoying after a while. And he had a guy with him who just stood there and smiled and nodded the whole time. Like an assistant or local parishioner. We felt bad for him. Anyway, it made our two-hour wait pass quickly.

Aberffraw is just a little village, with only this tea shop on one end of the main street and a pub at the other end of the street. That's pretty much it. So, once we get settled in our B&B and showered, we'll be having dinner at the pub. The next nearest restaurant is a few miles away.

Our day started with a great breakfast at the Cymyran Hotel. Probably the best breakfast yet. They offered omelettes and fresh-squeezed orange juice! You put whole oranges in a machine and it squeezes out the juice.

The weather forecast for today was cloudy, no rain, and windy, and it all held true. The stiff breeze was at our backs all day long, and it made for a chilly walk the entire day. Most of the first few miles were along sandy beaches, so I kept telling myself that we were beach combing and not hiking 12 miles with backpacks. Leslie found and saved a few big pieces of beach glass.

The walking was pretty flat. Some tall grass, some fields, some headlands, some gravel road, some beaches. We're getting far enough around the Isle of Anglesey now that we can see the mountains in Snowdonia on the mainland, off in the distance.

Around mile 10 we stopped for lunch on a little isolated beach. According to our guidebook, on the "secluded beach of Porth Cayfan" there is an ancient church dedicated to Saint Cayfan that was built in the seventh century! We also passed a prehistoric burial chamber from the Neolithic Period (2,000-4,000BC). Shit is old around here.

Okay, it is around 4:30pm and we are settled into our B&B at the Prince Llewelyn. Just had the best shower and best bath towel of the entire trip!!! The B&B is nice, but expensive, like $120US for one night. They will make a packed lunch tomorrow for £5 each, which we requested. There is a little sheet you fill out in advance for the lunches and there are four check boxes: ham, cheese, sandwich bread, and gluten-free bread. We both checked both the ham and cheese boxes, and then read the fine print at the bottom that said, "ham or cheese." Lame.

Today's hike was relatively easy. It went fairly quickly, under five hours, and we are all settled in for the night. We'll grab dinner at the pub at the end of the street. It's the only place in the village to eat. And then I need to get down to doing some computer work!! I've been slacking.

Leslie's Journal Entry:

Said goodbye to the grandpa shoes! Buried them in the bottom of our garbage can at the Queen Hotel in Porthmadog.Said hello to a gorgeous new pair of normal-looking hiking shoes.

Got over blisters in time to welcome shin splints. Hello, pain. I've missed you.

Thursday, September 7, 2017, Hiking Day 17
Aberffraw to Newborough, and on to Dwyran (Stable B&B)
14½ miles; Total – 203½ miles

We broke the 200-mile mark today!! We are planning to pay attention to lots of little milestones along the way…. Hundred-mile marks; our quarter, half, three-quarter, done for the entire trial marks; and our weekly marks, like one week completed, two weeks completed, etc. The halfway point at around 435 to 440 miles will be huge. As we did on the Southwest Coast Path, we took a photo of "200 Miles" drawn in the sand. We hit that point towards the end of our walk today, at around mile 12 for the day. Little goals like this give us something to look forward to and anticipate and provide a small sense of accomplishment in what, at this point, still seems like a completion goal that is a long way away.

I forgot to mention yesterday that the café we were hanging out at in Aberffraw, where we met the self-absorbed and loquacious priest the day before, was actually run by a non-profit that hired people with various disabilities. We realized right away that our waitress had some mental challenges when she asked, "So where in America do you live?" And Leslie replied, "Indiana." And our waitress said, "America must be such a big city."

She told us that she takes a bus to work every day from Mein Bridge. We asked her how long of a bus ride it is for her every day, and she replied, "Oh, I don't know. I just get on the bus, and then get off right here." She was really sweet. We'd noticed that a few of the other workers were dealing with some challenges as well. Knowing that we were supporting this great café made me feel a lot better about sitting there for two hours waiting for our B&B to open and listening to Father Talk-a-Lot for most of that time.

Today we knew we had a long hike ahead of us. Leslie claimed during a break we took at noon, around mile nine, that I'd failed to mention we were hiking 14½ miles today. I'm pretty sure I mentioned it a few times.

We check the weather forecast a lot on our phones, and today's forecast was rain beginning at 10am or 11am and continuing throughout the day and into the evening. The trail guide description for today said "relatively flat," so I wanted to walk as fast and as far as possible before the rain started. It was also a breezy and cloudy day.

The first few miles were along country lanes, and then we crossed a mile-long earthen dam that was holding back a body of water. It was an exposed and really windy section, so we were both anxious to get across. Then we hiked a good five miles through a forest, which was nice, and got us out of the wind. It felt odd to be going through the middle of a forest, away from the ocean, after walking along exposed seashore for the past 16 days.
The path was sometimes gravel and sometimes sandy, but overall pretty flat. So, we averaged three miles an hour when we were moving. We took a couple of nice snack breaks, sitting and stretching out on the grassy, sandy, comfortable ground.

At one point, Leslie went a little goofy, and started taking photos of our feet, and of my butt, and more of our feet. We didn't stop to eat the lunch we had packed until around 2pm, just as the wind picked up and it started to sprinkle. We were at the 13-mile mark for the day, the end of today's trail section, but we still had a mile and a half to go to the next village of Dwyran to our reserved B&B, The Stables. At our lunch stop, we decided to celebrate our 200-mile mark with a few photos and a hug and kiss.

We followed the path another mile and a half and then cut off the trail to get to Dwyran. I ended up taking us down a tractor path on a farmer's private property to get to a road that I thought would lead to our B&B. As we crossed his property, I saw the farmer on the other side of a pasture, so we just kept heading towards his house, and driveway, and ultimately the main road.

There was a locked gate to get from his driveway to the road, and just as I said to Leslie, "We are going to have to climb this stone wall to get to the road," I turned to see this very short, squatty, ruddy-faced older farmer walking towards us. Leslie and I both said at the same time, "We're lost." "Sorry for crossing your property," I added. The rest of the conversation went something like this:

Me: We're sorry. We got lost and are looking for The Stables B&B

Farmer: Huh. Where are you from? Are you Canadian?

Me: Yes. We're Canadian (sensing this was the right answer).

Farmer: Where in Canada? My dad lived in Canada for 20 years.

Me (I know Leslie is thinking, 'Oh shit…here we go.'): Oh. We're from just outside Toronto. Where did your dad live?

Farmer: Oh. Alberta. My wife and I have visited Canada lots of times. Calgary. The big rodeo there.

Me: Oh, that's quite a bit west of where we live.

Farmer: What's your names?

Me: Jon and Leslie.

Farmer: John you say? That's my name, too.

Me: What? Your name is Jon too?

Farmer: Yep. That's my name.

(We shake hands)

Me (teasingly): I don't believe you. That your name is Jon, just like mine.

Farmer: Yep it is. And I'll prove it (as he reaches over and rings his front door bell).

(An old lady comes to the door)

Me: This farmer I just met says his name is John.

Farmer's Wife: Yep. That's his name. John.

John the Farmer: These folks are from Canada. Where is it you're from again, Jon?

Me: Toronto. A long way from Alberta.
Leslie: Sorry again for accidentally going through your property.

John the Farmer: That was no accident. It was meant to be. I'm just glad you weren't English.

Me: You must be Welsh. Would you have come over to meet us with a gun if you knew we were English?

John the Farmer: No. We have a lot to thank them for. Like teaching us how to eat with our knife and fork.

Which is fucking hilarious, because every single English person we have seen in restaurants and cafes always eats with a fork permanently in one hand, and a knife permanently in the other hand. And these two utensils work in unison for every single bite of food. The knife helps the food onto the fork. It's so funny to watch. Even though 95 percent of the time, the fork would be sufficient to stab a piece of egg, or broccoli, or meat for example, the knife is always there to help it along. We've been making fun of this the whole trip, and here John the Farmer is making fun of them, too! It was brilliant.

Anyway, meeting John the Farmer, and his wife, his instant friendship and warm handshake, and his comment about "no accident," really made our day.

He said he thought he'd heard of The Stable, but didn't know where it was. His wife didn't know either. It turned out that it was only 200 yards down the same street!!

Don't ask me why I lied about being Canadian, without missing a beat. It's complicated.

Leslie's Journal Entry:

Supposed to be an easy walk today, but when you are trying to keep your beautiful new hikers from obtaining even a speck of dust, it gets a bit challenging.

It was a very pretty sunny day with stunning panoramic views. Plus, I got a new hat!

Still have shin splints which sucks—but, hey, I got a new hat.

Friday, September 8, 2017, Hiking Day 18
Dwyran to Llanfairpwll (Carreg Bran Hotel)
12 miles; Total – 215 miles

Yesterday I'd finished journaling before the events of the evening unfolded at the Stables. Mike, the owner, told us that we could come to the main part of the B&B anytime after 6pm. He and his wife, Michelle, offer a dinner menu since there are no restaurants in Dwyran. There were six or seven items on the menu and we both chose ground lamb with mint burgers and chips for a 7pm dinner. At around 6:30pm, I wandered over to have a beer (that Mike also told us were available in the main room) and do some computer work. The Wi-Fi in our room, which is in an adjacent building, was frustratingly non-existent.

When I walked over at 6:30pm, no one answered the door at the main house and the lights were turned off. I finally called the number on the door to see what was up, and Mike told me that there had been a family emergency, and that he and his wife were at the hospital for "precautionary measures." He said they'd be back by 7:45pm and we'd just have a late dinner. So, we sat on our bed and read and tried to access the internet through my poor cellphone signal.

Finally about 8:30pm we gave up on dinner and ate some cookies and cheese and crackers. At about 8:45pm, Mike came knocking on the door and told us his wife had been experiencing symptoms of a stroke or heart attack and that she was home from the hospital and lying down. He insisted that we still come over for dinner, even though we told him not to worry about it.

Tonight, was also the night that the new TV series that we'd been told about, *Safe House*, that was filmed in Treador Bay, was on at 9pm. It turned out that the main house in the show was a big stone mansion that we walked right past on the trail a few days ago. So, we ended up eating our lamb burgers, chips, and pie with ice cream in front of the TV in the B&B living room so that we could watch the first episode . . . which turned out to be a scary mystery.

Mike was a great host. We ate and watched TV until 10pm, and then went back to our room for the night. It was a weird evening to say the least.

Now, on to today. Great breakfast made by Michelle. I think Mike has taken a liking to us and an interest in our adventure. He seemed astonished that we still have 60 days of hiking left!!

We'd packed up, eaten breakfast, and were walking by 8:55am. It was a relatively easy and varied day of walking. The sun came in and out of the clouds all day. But no rain. We walked along some country lanes, and across some very wet and muddy pastures. It rained all night last night so there were some huge puddles and lots of wet grass. We successfully kept our feet fairly dry until we encountered a big wet area, with no way to walk around it. So, we tromped right through the water and completely soaked our shoes and socks, which stayed wet for the rest of the day.

We also walked a mile or so along the rocky seashore of Mendi Straits, and could easily see across to the other side, where we'll be walking tomorrow.

We were both pretty anxious to get our hiking done as early as possible today, to make it feel like we had the afternoon off. So, we walked faster than usual, and only took a couple of short rest and snack breaks the entire time. My legs and feet and joints ached today. I held off on taking any Advil for the first several miles, but finally took three at about 11am. Leslie has had a headache for the past few days which is such a bummer for her. But after walking a few hours, taking several Advil, and some kind of migraine pill that she'd gotten at a pharmacy, her headache finally started to recede around noon.

We walked right into Llanfairpwll. This is the village that really has a name that is a single word several lines long. A couple of people suggested that we visit the little train station where the sign with the name of the village stretches across the entire front of the station. And the sign alongside the railroad track is about 10 feet long. There is also a tourist store there with all kinds of souvenirs and other stuff. Mike was sure we'd find the trail maps that I've been seeking for the next section of the Wales Coast Path that doesn't have a guidebook printed yet. He also told Leslie she'd be able to buy a T-shirt there with the full name of the village on it.

Well, the souvenir store had neither thing we were looking for, but we stopped for lunch and then walked to the co-op grocery store to buy snacks, more Advil, and a few other items Leslie had been storing in her memory palace. Then it was another mile or so to the Carreg Bran Hotel, where we arrived by 3pm. The room was fine. The shower even better.

We both rinsed out our socks and undies, and stuffed sheets of a newspaper we'd bought for that reason into our shoes to help them dry out overnight. The hotel restaurant was really nice and we splurged on a nice dinner: salmon and chicken breasts. I spent a couple of hours before dinner in the bar doing some work and drinking a beer before Leslie came down to join me.

Tomorrow we walk back across the Menai Bridge that we first came across on August 28th, our seventh day of hiking, 12 days ago!! It has taken us 12 days to hike around the perimeter of the Isle of Anglesey. Once across the bridge, we'll be back on the mainland for the rest of our hike.

Lots of people plan for years to hike the 130-mile Isle of Anglesey Coastal Path. It's a big goal for U. K. hikers. We just finished it as only a small part of our overall hike. Just one of seven sections of the Wales Coast Path.

Leslie's Journal Entry:

SECTION THREE: LLYN PENINSULA

Bangor to Porthmadog

Saturday, September 9, 2017, Hiking Day 19
Llanfairpwll to Caernarfon
12 miles; Total – 227 miles

Other than getting charged at by a bull with very sharp-looking horns this morning, it was a pretty uneventful day. We were playing the "how long can we keep our feet dry" game when we entered a cow pasture on our way to the Menai Bridge from Llanfairpwll-gwyngyllgogerychchyrndrobwlllllantyjiliogogogoch.

The trail through the cow field was getting wetter and muddier and we reached a part where a small stream had developed from last night's rain. So, in looking for the least wet way to get through the most wet section, I walked upfield, closer to a black bull with big dark horns, who was standing next to a brown cow.

When I got about 10 feet away from the bull, he started to charge me, and then suddenly stopped. Like a bluff. I quickly conceded the dry shoe game and veered into a very swampy section of the pasture while talking to the black bull in my calmest voice. I briefly turned my back on the bull to get out of there as fast as I could, and he charged me again. So, I spun around, scared to death, and yelled something like, "Hoaaa, bull," and waved my arms with my hiking poles attached. Leslie let out a shriek, too, at that moment. The bull stopped. I quickly sloshed through a 50-foot section of calf-deep water and mud, and that was that.

The next problem came when deciding which direction Leslie should go. I ended up climbing over a low stone wall to get out of the pasture and onto the beach. So, Leslie ended up backtracking a bit, and climbed over a higher stone wall to avoid the bull and get to the beach. In retelling the story, Leslie claimed that I was almost gored to death. But I'm pretty sure it wasn't that close.

Otherwise, today was a fair amount of road and paved bike trail walking, other than the first mile and a half miles from the Carreg Bran Hotel, in the town whose name I will never write again, then over the Menai Bridge.

The weather report was for 80 to 90 percent chance of rain every hour from 8am to 4pm. So, Leslie started out in full raingear and I had my raincoat on as well. But it really only sprinkled three or four times, and only for a few minutes each time. And then once, as we were entering Caernarfon at the end of our hike, a hard pounding rain came out of nowhere, but only lasted 10 minutes or so. So, it turned out that most of the day it was pretty nice hiking weather.

We had a little snack break at a wet picnic table we happened upon. And then stopped around noon for lunch in a pub in the little village of Fellinheli. We stopped at the little post office there first to mail home Trail Guide #2 and some maps, but it had closed at noon (today is Saturday) and we arrived at 12:05pm.

I had a dumb lunch. I'm not sure what I was thinking. I ordered a bowl of cooked vegetables, a small salad, and a cold-smoked salmon sandwich which was not very good. Leslie had a homemade vegie burger, salad, and fries, and proceeded to fart her way through the remaining five miles of our hike.

Caernarfon is known for a huge castle and castle walls that still surround the main part of the town. It was built in the mid-1200s by Kind Edward I, and is still almost totally intact. Pretty impressive. It is a cute town with lots of options for places to eat, which is pretty much how we judge towns, 19 days into this hike. I was on a quest to find hiking maps for the current Section Three of the Wales Coast Path, and especially for Section Four coming up, for which we don't even have a guidebook, since one hasn't been published yet. The guidebook for Section Four was supposed to come out in September of 2017 (this month), but a lady in a small bookstore today looked it up and found out that now it is due to be published in October. I was really excited to find the trail maps that we'll need for that section of the trail that has no guidebook. That made me very happy.

So, we bought maps, walked completely around the castle, stopped for a beer, and had an early dinner. Usually, once we are done with our hike for the day, we don't do any extra walking around or sightseeing. We just shower and lay in bed. But today, because of the map-quest and interesting castle, we were on our feet for an extra couple of hours.

I want to write a little bit about helpful people. Last night at the hotel we were trying to book places to stay a few days from now, and had no cell service. And I was just having a generally hard time finding places to stay. I asked the lady at the front desk if she could place a call for me, and she completely took over our hotel search, successfully booking places for us for the next three nights. Super helpful and friendly, and willing to give us a hand.

Today at the pub for lunch there were two guys at the bar who started asking us questions, and immediately offered all kinds of advice and helpful information once they found out what we were doing.

While we were walking after lunch today, and nearing Caernarfon, an older gentleman with a little daypack stopped us with, "You look like you are far from home." We ended up having the nicest talk. He has hiked all over the U. K. and done some long-distance hikes like the El Camino in Spain, which he has hiked twice. I told him about my map-quest and he had several suggestions of where to inquire. He also gave us a lot of info about the next several days of hiking and what we'll be encountering.

While we were talking with him, a local lady who was walking her dog,stopped and she, too, helped with ideas of where to find maps, and directions for several places in town. Both were very friendly people, and very willing to help two total strangers. Some people would attribute these helpful people to being "trail angels" or to God helping us along the way. But I attribute it to nice people who are just being nice, and who want to help others or might look or sound like they need a little help. These are the people and events that stand out in my mind as I think back over our first 19 days of hiking in Wales.

Leslie's Journal Entry:

Sunday, September 10, 2017, Hiking Day 20
Caernarfon to Trefor
17½ miles (Longest day so far); Total – 244½ miles

We did it! 17½ miles today.

And almost all of it done while walking headlong into a stiff wind. The first 10 miles were along coastal country lanes and a few miles of foot paths with no protection from the wind. It consistently blew 20-25 mph and gusted above that. It was relentless and in our faces all day long. Neither of us talked much. Leslie did say several times, "Just put your head down and go." So, we did.

It sprinkled on and off between 9am and 11am. And then there was a brief heavy soaking rain right at the end as we entered Trefor. Otherwise, it was just chilly and really annoyingly windy. It wasn't any fun walking at all!

The time did seem to pass quickly, however. We started walking from our B&B in Caernarfon at 8:30am, and only stopped briefly once for Leslie to put on her rain pants after about 90 minutes. When we got to the little seaside village of Dinn Dinlle, there thankfully was a little café open. The wind was really howling at that point, and we'd just finished walking a section that was right along the water and along a raised walkway, so the wind was really gusting and blowing us around.

But when we went into the cafe to get some coffee and cocoa and carrot cake, it was already 11:35am. We'd been walking for three straight hours, which surprised both of us. And we'd already gone a little over halfway (nine miles).

The coffee was probably the best I'd had the entire trip. And it was so nice to be inside and out of the wind for a bit. It was almost entirely road and paved path walking today. It's an issue for landowners allowing (or not allowing) hikers to pass through their fields and property, and apparently this section has very few agreeable landowners. I'm reminded that the official Wales Coast Path was only designated as such in 2012 (five years ago), linking several long-standing paths into one contiguous trail. But linking everything together means that there are still several sections where no actual trail exists. Every year though, it will keep getting better and better.

Leslie just said, "Don't forget to write about our new favorite hiking game." So up until now our two favorite hiking games are *Guess What Time It Is* and *Guess How Much the Meal We Just Ate Cost*. But today, as we walked on a paved hiking path that paralleled a busy road for seven miles, Leslie suggested a new game that she said that she and Tyler used to play. The game was to guess the color of the car that was coming up the road behind us, before it passed. The rules were that you couldn't turn around and look until it passed; you could only guess the same color two cars in a row; and we both couldn't guess the same color at the same time. So, Leslie would yell (over the wind), "Blue!" and I'd yell, "Black!" and then when a car passed us from behind, we'd see who won. Sometimes we'd yell three or four colors in quick succession if there were a few cars in a row racing past us.

The game was fun, and kind of stressful.

Leslie can turn anything into a game. At one point, I was ahead eight to three! But then she almost caught up. I think I won 10 to eight. But that took up like 30 minutes of walking, and took our minds off of our aching feet. I ate a total of six Advil today. Leslie probably had the same.

At one point, we passed a little stone wall that was dedicated to Saint Bueno, who in the 1200s brought a woman back from the dead by reattaching her head that had been cut off. Apparently, after he did that, this well sprung up and stories abound of how its healing water cured children of epilepsy. Saint Bueno also brought several other people back from the dead as well. So, we stopped for a minute while Leslie dabbed some of the healing water into her ears. It was worth a try.

Other than the coffee shop, the *Guess the Color of the Car* game, and Saint Bueno's well, it was a pretty uneventful hike. We were able to walk without our full packs today, which made a huge difference. There is no lodging in Trefor, our endpoint for today. Apparently, the only hotel burned down a few years ago. So, when we got to the little village, we stopped in a dinky 7/11-type store, which was literally the only commercial place we saw in the village.

Thankfully, the mini mart was open, because when we arrived it was pouring down rain. We got coffee from a hot coffee machine, and coincidentally, the only taxi driver in town was shopping in the little market. So, he ran his groceries home, and then drove us back to Caernarfon. He dropped us off in the town square next to the castle. What had taken us exactly six hours to hike at a fast and non-stop pace, took 25 minutes to drive by car.

I forget to mention that we did stop for lunch around 1pm. We spotted at a little rural stone bus stop out in the country that had a bench and was out of the wind. We made salami, cheese, and mustard sandwiches, and ate barbecue corn Bugles, and some chocolate for dessert. It was so nice to be out of the wind for a few minutes.

Back home, we went to the Black Boy Pub for a beer and then just decided to eat dinner there, too, even though it was only 4:30pm, so we could just go home afterwards, shower, and then not have to leave again. We ordered "Cornish Pudding" which consisted of roast beef, peas, carrots, and mash, all inside a big baked crust with gravy poured over the top. We split that massive meal and had a couple of salads. Perfect.

In our room, I spent at least two hours trying to set up our lodging for the next four or five nights. The towns we have coming up are small and the few lodging options were all booked up. No Airbnbs. Two of the day endpoints aren't even in villages, and one just ends at a public beach parking lot. So definitely no place to stay there, and no grocery store or places to eat. I eventually pieced a couple of places together, but it was a pain finding them and we are going to have to do a lot of taxiing back and forth between lodging and trailheads.

As I lay here in bed, it is around 9pm and my feet are throbbing. Too much pavement walking (17½ miles). Leslie is sound asleep, but the last thing she did was take a few Advil because here feet are throbbing, too.

Leslie's Journal Entry:

Monday, September 11, 2017, Hiking Day 21
Trefor to Nefyn (and on to Morfa Nefyn)
10 miles; Total – 254½ miles

We are sitting in a small pub in Morfa Nefyn, and it feels like home. The name of the pub is Y-Bryncynan. The second we walked in we were greeted by a local guy. The local Nefyn cab driver was at the bar having a beer. I saw him get out of his taxi when we walked in, and we'll need the phone number for a taxi to call at the end of our hike to Colman Bay tomorrow. So, I introduced myself and we hit it off. We'll call him tomorrow afternoon at the end of our hiking day. I said, "It's always a good sign when your taxi driver is at the pub having a beer." Some other guy at the bar said, "Yeah, you don't want a tense driver. You want him relaxed."

Another guy has come over to our table several times to tell us local bits of historical knowledge. He taught us "shoe-my," Welsh for "How are you?" and "nos-dah," which is "goodbye." (Those are phonetic spellings.) I have no idea how they're spelled in Welsh.

Y-Bryncynan is the kind of place where the local fishermen and other workers come at the end of the day. All men at the bar. I don't see any women. And everyone is speaking Welsh. It is so cool to be in places where everyone is speaking Welsh. It's definitely the first language of everyone here.

We got our asses kicked by the wind today!!!

We hiked for a couple of hours up on a high exposed ridge. No trees or shrubs to block the wind. We had another great breakfast at our Cardiff Guest House and then grabbed our taxi at 8:45am and were back in Trefor by 9am ready to walk. I'd left my hiking poles in the little store at Trefor when we stopped in the rain yesterday, and thankfully they were still there this morning when we returned.

I had a small package of maps and the guidebook for Anglesey to mail home, but the little post office in Trefor that opens at 9am wasn't open at 9:15am, so I kept the stuff in my pack, and we headed out rather than waiting around.

The trail led straight up a steep and narrow paved road that turned into a steep and narrow gravel road, and then eventually a path to the top of a saddle. It was fairly steep and took about an hour to get up on the saddle. The views back behind us were nothing short of spectacular! The clouds hung just above our heads as we had great views in both directions. It was windy on the way up, but once we crested the saddle, the wind hit us full force. It must have been blowing 40mph consistently. Enough to make it difficult to walk in a straight line, and the gusts definitely knocked us back a step or two, or off the path altogether.

At one point it started to rain, and the rain hitting our faces and my legs felt like hundreds of little needles coming at us sideways. We walked in that wind for about two hours straight. At one point we lost the trail and had to backtrack a bit. Which was frustrating. At some points it was all we could do to keep moving forward, and we had to stand right next to each other and yell to be heard.

At one point, Leslie started laughing out loud it was so crazy. That was when it started to rain. Later in the day, towards the end of our hike, she said, "This sounds kind of crazy, but I like it better when we were getting blown around. It made the hiking a lot more interesting."

The scenery remained stunning all the way into Nefyn, which is the end of today's trail section in the guidebook. There was no place to stay in Nefyn (that had an available room) so we went to the Spar grocery store, mailed my package, and bought some sandwich meat and chips for tomorrow's lunch. And then we walked a mile and a half to Morfa Nefyn and the Fairway Guest House. It is kind of along the way we need to go tomorrow. At least the first mile is. So, that's one less mile that we have to walk tomorrow.

I forgot to mention that for lunch today we stopped alongside a small church that was built in the 1600s in honor of Saint Bueno, the healer of cut-off heads. The church was surrounded by cemetery headstones (no pun intended) and crypts. We hunkered down alongside one of the church walls to get out of the wind, and to make and eat our sandwiches. Leslie is really enamored by cemeteries, so she spent several minutes reading headstone inscriptions. She found two who had died in 1774 and 1747.

The Fairway Guest House is older and is operated, or maybe owned, by an older couple. The attached restaurant isn't open tonight and it appears that we are the only people staying here in one of their 10 rooms. So, after unpacking, doing a little laundry in the sink, and resting our weary bones, we walked for three-quarters of a mile up the road to the pub I mentioned at the beginning of this entry.

After beers and dinner, we said, "Nos-dah," as we left.

A word about doing laundry. Today was the end of our third week of hiking. Both of us basically cycle through two outfits. Leslie maybe has three. So, we end up wearing the same things over and over again. We've been to a laundromat once, and then two other times the place where we were staying had a laundry service. One time the manager just did our laundry for free.

Otherwise, one or the other of us is rinsing out at least one item every night. Usually a pair of socks or underwear. Getting things to dry is the real problem. Virtually all of the places where we've stayed haven't turned their radiator heaters on yet for the fall. So, the rooms aren't heated. And it has been raining on and off the past week, so hanging clothes off our packs to dry while we hike hasn't worked too well either.

This afternoon, since we are at the Fairway for two nights, we both handwashed several things in the sink, including the T-shirt and pair of shorts I've been wearing for the past five days, probably longer. We also asked the landlady if she could turn on the heat. So, our stuff should hopefully be dry by tomorrow night. We'll check at the B&B where we are staying in a couple of nights to see if they do laundry for guests. It is such a treat when we have a laundry option. Most of the towns where we've stayed don't have laundromats, and the few that did closed at 5pm or aren't anywhere near where we are staying. So, it's mostly handwashing with a once-a-week washing machine.

Leslie's Journal Entry:

Tuesday, September 12, 2017, Hiking Day 22
Morfa Nefyn to Porth Colman
11 miles; Total – 265½ miles

Last night at the Y-Bryncynan pub, the guy that taught us how to say "shoe-my" and "nos-dah," we found out today from our taxi driver (the one having a drink at the pub last night between rides) that this guy is a famous Welsh pop singer. Apparently in the 1970s, when the taxi driver was just a lad, Dewi Pws ("Dewi" is Welsh for "David") was in a nationally known pop band called the Purple Teapots (or whatever the Welsh words for "purple teapot" are). The taxi driver said on our drive to our starting point for the day, "I never dreamed as a kid that I'd ever meet Dewi Pws. And now I live in the same town, and drink at the same pub as he does." Apparently, Dewi is also a movie actor, and continues to put out solo albums. Dewi mentioned last night that he's been learning how to play the banjo "Earl Scruggs" style. And when I Googled his name this afternoon, there were some YouTube videos of him playing the banjo at various music festivals.

Our taxi driver picked us again up in Porth Colman this afternoon at 2pm when we'd finished our 11 miles for the day. A super nice guy. He told us all about Dewi Pws, and then offered to stop at a little grocery store as we got back into Morfa Nefyn, at no extra cost, so we could run in and get some food for lunch and hiking snacks for tomorrow. His wife was working at the store, so we met her, too. He also picked us up and drove us to dinner tonight at The Cliffs, a nice restaurant in Morfa Nefyn that is perched on a cliff above the sea. It's about a mile from our hotel, and we had no interest in walking there, or back.

We had great dinners of sea bass and salmon, and are finishing off the night with a couple of gin and tonics and a freshly baked, still-warm brownie with two scoops of ice cream. We'll walk it off during our 14 miles tomorrow!!

It is pissing down rain right now (8pm) and has been for a while. I caught a glimpse of the weather on the TV in the hotel lobby and it said "gale force winds" sweeping through the center of the U.K. tomorrow, and high winds on the north coast! I just checked my weather app and it shows the rain is stopping by morning, but I think it's going to be really windy!!

We walked past a little secluded bay today and Leslie noticed the head of a seal or sea otter popping out of the water, so we stopped to watch. The longer we stood there, the more heads started popping up and looking at us. Then, once we really focused in, we realized there were 20 to 25 harbor seals down there, maybe half swimming around in the protected bay, and the other half up on the rocks and the rocky seashore trying to warm up in the occasional sun that kept poking through the clouds. There was no way to get down to the seals, so they were completely safe and protected. We eventually heard a few of the harbor seals barking, so I started barking back.

The seas were still pretty riled up today, and the wind blew steady all day long, but only 10 to 15mph. And the sun was out quite a lot. It ended up being really pleasant hiking weather, amplified by not having to carry our backpacks, and only needing to hike 11 miles.

The scenery as we walked southwest along the Llyn Peninsula was amazing. Black jagged, rocky cliffs, deep blue-green ocean all churned up by the wind, and rich green pasture land up above. The sun ducked in and out of the clouds all day. The entire hike was stunning. We didn't pass through any big towns or touristed beaches like we did on parts of Anglesey and all along the north coast of Wales. This coastal section of Wales is more remote and less populated. Less touristy. I like it.

Leslie's Journal Entry:

Reflections:
1. Do not blow snot upwind of your husband. He doesn't like it.

Wednesday, September 13, 2017, Hiking Day 23
Porth Colman to Aberderon
14 miles; Total – 279½ miles

The weather forecast we heard for today was for high coastal winds and occasional showers. For a 14-mile day with lots of ups and downs, we were mentally prepared for a really hard day. Our taxi driver, who is becoming a friend, especially now that we know his name—Griffin—drove us from Morfa Nefyn to Porth Colman, where we left off yesterday. He then picked us up at the end of our hike today in Aberderon. When he met us in Aberderon, he drove us on to the village of Abersoch because we weren't able to book any place to stay in Aberderon.

When Griffin dropped us off at Porth Colman, he agreed to keep our backpacks in his trunk for the day, as he ran his taxi service, so once again, we were able to hike with only my jam-packed 10-pound daypack full of our lunch and snacks, two liters of water, raincoats and rain pants, maps, baby powder in case one of our butts starts chaffing again, trail guidebook, and of course, Advil.

The route today really reminded us of parts of the Southwest Coast Path. There were lots of big climbs and descents, and a few extended climbs. And, over 14 miles, it was pretty tiring. We were both dragging towards the end of the day. It was windy all day, and blowing into our faces as it came off the Irish Sea, but it wasn't unbearable. The sun came out at about 11am, and poked in and out of the clouds for the rest of the day. So, the hiking weather turned out way better than we expected, and the scenery was killer. We both agreed it was the most fantastic day of scenery yet! Lots of high viewpoints where we could see for miles and miles in every direction. Crashing waves. High, steep black cliffs. A couple of times, after walking along miles of steep black rocky cliffs, we'd come upon a beautiful hidden cove with a perfect sandy beach. And of course, absolutely no one around.

Mid-morning, we saw the first person we've seen during the entire 23 days so far who was carrying a full pack and coming towards us from the south. Once I got up to her, I realized it was the young German woman we had passed several times during our first two to three days of hiking. We'd nicknamed her Ingfrid (Jon's nickname) and Gweny (Leslie's nickname), since we'd never learned her real name.

So, this time, we actually stopped to talk with her. She was walking the wrong direction, which was odd, but she said she was having a hard time finding hostels to stay in, so she took a bus across the peninsula and now was hiking backwards towards Caernarfon. She has been carrying a tent and sleeping bag the entire time, but said she's only used it three times because of the winds and rain. She's afraid she'll snap a tent pole in the rain, and then be screwed.

So, she's using it just for emergency overnights.

"Ingfrid" told us that she'd started out planning to through-hike the entire Wales Coast Path (so she's now the only other through-hiker, besides us, that we've seen on the trip), but she seemed unsure now if she would complete the whole thing given how hard it has been for her to camp and find cheap hostels to stay in. We told her our plans and said we hoped to see her further down the trail once she finishes this section that she's hiking backwards. It just remined us again how apparently few through-hikers there are on the Wales Coast Path this year.

Around 11am, we stopped for our first break at the only public/commercial place in the entire 14-mile day, a little snack shop on Whistling Sands Beach. It was so nice to get out of the wind and inside a building. We bought hot lattes and a scone with clotted cream and jelly. So good!! Neither of us wanted to get up and start walking in the wind again. And I calculated that we'd only walked five and a half or six miles in those first three hours, which was disheartening.

Although the scenery was amazing and motivating, and kept my mind off of our aching knees from all of the steep downhills, we didn't find a decent lunch spot that was mostly out of the wind until around 1:30pm. Same old meat and cheese white bread sandwich, and salt and vinegar chips. We had tangerines today, too, but we need to think of some new lunch foods.

The sun was out the last few miles and there were several day hikers on the trail coming from Aberderon. We finished at 3:30pm, hiking for seven and a half hours with really only those two breaks. Aberderon is a very cute, small but touristy seaside village. We saw several little restaurants, two pubs, and two or three coffee shops. One coffee shop and a bakery open at 7:30am, so when we get our ride back here tomorrow morning to start walking, maybe we'll grab a cup of good coffee first. Good coffee has been pretty hard to come by, and definitely not served at the B&Bs.

We both have our minds set on getting to Porthmadog on Saturday or Sunday (today is Wednesday). It's a big town that we know has two camping stores (we have a short list of things we need to get), a laundromat, and a bookstore where I can hopefully buy some kind of trail guidebook for the next section of the Coast Path. The official guide for the upcoming section hasn't been published yet, but there is another older, less detailed book that will help somewhat. So anyways, we're both excited about getting to Porthmadog in a few days. Something to look forward to.

It's 9:10pm. We've been in bed for an hour already, have bellies full of Indian food, and throbbing feet. That's long-distance hiking in Wales.

Leslie's Journal Entry:

Reflections:
1. If snot were a natural moisturizer, I would look 10 years younger by the end of this trip.

Thursday, September 14, 2017, Hiking Day 24
Aberderon to Hell's Mouth Bay (Angorfa B&B)
11 miles; Total – 290½ miles

The best part of today was the full, end-to-end rainbow we saw arching over the sea at dinner time. The second best part was seeing these two identical white horses that appeared on the trail in front of us, as we walked above a high, steep cliff. Two beautiful and identical white horses with an ocean backdrop. It was almost like two magical unicorns appeared out of nowhere. My third best part of the day was seeing up ahead several hundred steep stair-steps dropping straight down from our trail to a remote beach, getting psyched up to go all the way down them (knowing we'd have to come right back up again), and then realizing that the hundreds of steep steps weren't actually part or our trail. My fourth best part of the day was walking four miles along Hell's Mouth Beach as fast as we could, so we wouldn't get caught between the rising tide and the steep cliffs, and after finishing the four miles, stopping for a late lunch, sitting in the sand. Which led to my fifth best part of the day, which was realizing that where we'd stopped for lunch was only a few hundred yards from the end of our hiking day. I'm still not sure why we stopped for lunch so close to the end of this trail section?

My sixth best part of the day was thinking about how amazing it is to be doing what we are doing right now. And being able to do it with Leslie. She's been amazing. No complaints (almost). Just willing to get up day after day after day, and put on her very stinky hiking shoes and socks, and just getting it done. Every day.

I may have written about this already, but stinky things drive Leslie crazy. And her hiking shoes stink!! She's only had them for, what, three weeks now? But between stepping in that big cow pie a while back, getting them soaked by walking through low wet areas, wet grass, and mud puddles every day, added to the stink of hiking in them all day long; she can't get the smell out of them. It's her quest for the Holy Grail. Trying to find a way to get the stink out of her shoes.

Oh, by the way, my seventh best part of the day was eating Thai food for dinner. And, last but not least, number eight was watching the second episode of *Safe House* on BBC1, the show we started watching last Thursday. It's only the second time we've turned on a TV in three and a half weeks.

Leslie's Journal Entry:

When we got in the taxi this morning, after a few minutes the cab driver put his window down a bit, even though it was freezing outside. I think we smell.

We are waiting for the taxi at the end of the hike today when I think that I just sat down in dog shit. Then, while tying my shoes, I realize it is my shoes! I hate these things.

We get in the taxi and after a minute, a totally different driver, puts her window down. It is me. OMG.

But, breathtaking beauty for several days now. Worth the stink.

Friday, September 15, 2017, Hiking Day 25
Hell's Mouth Parking Lot to Llanbedrog (Angorfa B&B)
14 miles; Total – 304½ miles

Rain, rain go away . . . you suck.

We are soaked, and I've been lying in bed for the last three hours, and am still chilled. The stupid weather forecast.

I check three different weather apps every morning, including one called "U.K. Weather," which today showed a 50 percent chance of some scattered showers until late morning, along with a 20mph wind all day. We've basically had the same forecast every day for the last week, and we'll get a little shower that lasts a couple of minutes a few times in the morning. It usually quits right when we stop to get our raincoats and pack covers on.

This morning we caught a taxi back to Hell's Mouth Beach after eating our 27th straight variation on the "traditional Welsh breakfast," and started hiking under an overcast sky. After hiking for just a few minutes along the beach, I was like "What the hell, I'll just go ahead and put on my raincoat and pack cover before it starts. Usually, I wait until after it's been raining hard for a few minutes, hoping it'll just stop, and then I end up getting soaked by the time I put my raincoat on.

On days like today, I put everything in Ziploc bags . . . map, guidebook, wallet, phone, lunch, snacks. . . . Everything gets its own Ziploc bag. And our clothes are already all in dry bags. Anyway, within a minute of putting on our raincoats it was pouring rain. Big fat raindrops. Just a heavy, soaking rain that blew sideways from the wind. And it sure seemed like there was some ice crystals in some of those big raindrops.

It was funny, because just after we started walking, we had to cross a stream. Both of us walked up and down the bank, trying to find a way to cross without getting our feet wet so early in the day. Dry shoes and socks have been a rare luxury the past week or so. I found a way across, and only lefty got wet. Leslie ended up taking her shoes and socks off, and crossing barefoot.

And 10 minutes later, water was streaming down our bare legs and filling our shoes. And an hour later, we were just purposely splashing through the biggest puddles we could find, as the rain just kept pouring down.

At one point, I realized that my right side was completely soaked, since the wind was blowing from that direction. Then the trail turned 90 degrees, and my front got drenched. Then it turned 90 degrees again, and my left side got soaked, too. About an hour into the rainstorm, Leslie announced that her underwear was still dry. Apparently her raincoat hung down far enough?

The whole day we were both on the verge of hypothermia. Around 11:30am, the rain stopped long enough for my nylon pants to almost completely dry, and then it started raining again. It rained on and off until we stopped in Llanbedrog around 3:30pm.

The big highlight of the day was that around mile 10, we walked right past our B&B and right through Abersoch, where we've been staying. Around 1:30pm we stopped in a pub for lunch and had an over-priced raw hamburger with "gourmet chips" which were the same damn steak fries we've had a dozen times.

Actually, the real and only true highlight of the day is that we hit our 300-mile mark today on our 25th day of hiking. So, by both mileage, and number of days walking, we are about one-third done with the Wales Coast Path. We etched "300 Miles" in the sand and planted Monkey Face in the middle for our celebratory photo.

Nothing else worth writing about. It just wasn't a fun day. Nothing fun about it. And 14 miles is still 14 miles!! It never seems to get any shorter. I can't wait for the sun to come out one of these days!! The locals have been saying that this is the worst September they've had in a decade. Today a lady told us, "This is Winter weather." Here's hoping for an unseasonably nice October!

Leslie's Journal Entry:

I woke up lethargic, headachy, and just not into it today. The six hours of pelting rain and 20mph winds did wonders to lighten the ol' mood.

Raw hamburger for lunch—that helped, too.

Saturday, September 16, 2017, Hiking Day 26
Llanbedrog to 2½ miles before Criccieth (Queen's Hotel in Porthmadog)
13 miles; Total – 317½ miles

The highlight of today was that about two hours after we started walking, we entered the town of Pwllheli (pronounced "Pookelly," I think). Our intention was to find a grocery store to pick up some lunch supplies, but instead . . . we found a Subway! I've been talking about getting a Subway sandwich for weeks! We were there around 10am, so I had a breakfast sandwich, and we both got Subway subs, chips, and chocolate chip cookies that we carried along with us for a later lunch. The subs were a bit soggy by the time we ate them. But I was happy.

The low point of the day is that around noon, Leslie started developing shin splints. Shin splints!! A dull throbbing pain in her left shin, with occasional sharp shooting pains up her leg. The pain stayed with her for the rest of the day, and she limped noticeably for the last few miles. It was hard to see her in pain and I kept making what probably ended up being too many annoying suggestions.

There were a few times that we wanted to stop for lunch, and a break, but it would start to rain. It seemed like every time we had selected a spot to stop, it would start to rain again. I was actually getting really frustrated with the rain today. It has been a week, probably more, of rain on and off every single day. And a good stiff wind on most of those days, too. Just getting a little tired of it.

When we stopped for the day, about two and a half miles before Criccieth, we called a taxi and he took us to the Queen's Hotel in Porthmadog.

Today was the day we've been anticipating for well over a week. We had the late afternoon all planned out and had gone over it in our minds and aloud a dozen times. We actually started hiking this morning at our earliest time yet, 7:50am, so we could get to Porthmadog with plenty of time.

We dropped our stuff in the hotel and walked straight to two camping stores in town, the first ones we've encountered since Leslie bought her hiking shoes a few weeks ago. On Leslie's shopping list: new "un-stinky" shoes, warm hat, gloves, and a long sleeve hiking shirt, and then I wanted to get a couple of maps for the next section. We also wanted to go to Brower's Books to buy a guidebook for the next section; go to a pharmacy to pick up a few things; get some newspaper to stuff into our soaking wet shoes. So, by the end of the day we'd pretty much accomplished everything on our list. Oh, and we found a local laundromat and I went there after dinner and did a big stinky load of laundry, while Leslie stayed back and rested her aching shin.

It ended up being a good day overall. We got a lot accomplished. We have all clean clothes, and some new shoes, and are snug in bed at the end of a 13-mile day on our 26th straight day of hiking.

Everyone at home has seemed to enjoy the photos I send every day or two. And Seth has been especially supportive, particularly when we've had a hard day.

Leslie's Journal Entry:

Sunday, September 17, 2017, Hiking Day 27
2½ miles before Criccieth to Porthmadog (Queen's Hotel)
9 miles; Total – 326½ miles

Today was only nine miles without packs. And it was the first day in over a week that it did not rain!! It was perfect hiking weather. We started by sleeping in a bit, and then had breakfast at our Queen's Hotel before grabbing our pre-arranged 9:15am taxi and heading to the spot we left off at yesterday, about three miles before Criccieth. Unfortunately, the Queen's Hotel is the only lodging in all of Porthmadog that had an available room this weekend, and apparently has available rooms for a reason.

The people are nice, the room was clean, and the breakfast was typical and fine. But there are lots of little details that need attending too. Like yesterday when we got here, the young lady behind the bar led us up three flights of stairs in the dark to get to our room. The walls need paint and the outside looks shabby and uncared for.

This morning, when we came down for breakfast, I had to poop. I didn't want to poop in our room, because our toilet doesn't flush very well and all of the toilet paper stays in the bowl. Anyway, I walk down a dark hallway to the restaurant bathroom, couldn't find any light switches, and go into a bathroom stall in the pitch dark. So, I go out and ask some guy in a paint spattered T-shirt, who I saw coming out of the kitchen (the cook), if he could help me turn on the light in the bathroom. Back to the stall, the room is so tiny I have to put one foot up on the toilet bowl so I can squeeze in and close the stall door. I sit down, and notice just in time, that there is no toilet paper. Not even a toilet paper dispenser roll holder. Nothing. So, back to the kitchen to find the paint-spattered guy. "Toilet paper, please?" He replies, "You're really making me work this morning." Apparently. He rummages around in a closet and eventually hands me a huge, like 10,000 sheet roll. One of those huge rolls you find in an airport bathroom. Anyway, a few little details would really improve the Queen's Hotel.

Our taxi driver this morning was the guy that picked us up yesterday afternoon, Criccieth Taxi. The driver, John, is a jolly chubby guy. Super nice, and seemed so happy to see us again this morning. We also saw him about an hour after he dropped us off, after we'd hiked back into Criccieth. We stopped in a famous Wales ice cream and coffee place—Cadwaladers—and as we sat and drank our mid-morning lattes, here he walked in with his elderly mother.

And again, he seemed so happy to see us again. It was like bumping into an old friend. It rarely happens on this walk that we bump into someone we've already met.

The tough part of today is that Leslie seems to have developed some nasty shin splints in her left leg. They started yesterday and sent sharp pains up her leg all day today. So, she used her hiking pole more than usual to support her left side, and limped through the entire nine miles. We weren't carrying our packs today and the trail was pretty flat, so that all helped. But I'm nervous about if and how this is going to heal, and hate seeing her wince in pain. We can definitely take a day or two off, if we need to, but right now she's saying "no." She read up on shin splints last night and is massaging the area, and put a big bag of ice on her shins for a couple of hours after we finished our hike today. Tomorrow we go 11 miles with our big packs back on, so again, I'm a little nervous. It took us about five and a half hours to only go nine miles today, so we may have to adjust our mileage over the coming days.

With the fairly clear day today, and high clouds, we could see a lot of the Snowdonia mountains, which were beautiful. Around mile five we hiked a two-mile stretch along a beautiful sandy beach (apparently the longest sandy beach in Wales). With the tide out as we walked, the sand stretched a quarter to a half-mile from the sand dunes out to the water. There were lots of people out walking, picnicking, throwing tennis balls to their dogs, and a few even swimming in the chilly water. So, we enjoyed people watching as Leslie limped along.

Leslie wore her brand-new hiking shoes today. She loves them! But she was nervous about getting them wet and muddy. She's so paranoid about having stinky shoes again. At one point, we went completely off the trail on a big detour so we could avoid a huge deep puddle that we couldn't get around. She took her shoes and socks off to cross two small shallow streams today, which worked just fine. Righty and lefty stayed dry all day.

Back to the beach for a second. When we first got to the big beach, there were two old geezers racing their motorized scooters up and down the beach, and even into the shallow water. They looked like they were having a blast.

At one point today, as we rounded a small headland, we were already off the trail because we'd avoided that one huge wet area and had to go a completely different way. Anyway, on the other side of this headland was the two-mile beach. I cut off from our alternate route, and clambered down some rocks to get right back to the beach, the shortest route. But Leslie wasn't comfortable climbing down because it was too steep. So, she went around a different way, and I waited, and waited, and waited. No Leslie.

I walked a ways down the beach and found where the trail hit the beach and then I started backtracking. I was worried that she wouldn't find the trail from the detour she'd taken, or would try going back to where I'd left her, or who knows what? Anyway, after about 45 minutes I spotted her way up on the ridge, heading down the trail. I was worried that she'd be pissed because I'd taken the rocky short cut, but when we finally got to each other, she was all happy and good-natured.

After Leslie iced her leg this afternoon, we walked to the Purple Moose Brewery and had a couple of pints of local brews, downed some dinner, and now we're back at the Queen's Hotel, sitting downstairs having a nightcap because we can't get internet in our room. (Another strike against the place.)

Leslie's Journal Entry:

Day #1 - Official Start of the Wales Coast Path

Day #5 – Conwyn Estuary

Day #9 – Isle of Anglesey nearing our 100 mile mark

Day #10 - Nearing Amlwch on the Isle of Anglesey

Day #11 – Heading to Cemaes

*Day #14 – Taking a break while hiking around
Holy Head Peninsula*

Day #14 – Drying out after a wet day

Day #15 – Llanfairyneubwll

Day #16 – Nearing Aberffraw

Day #17 – 200-mile mark

Day #18 – Welcome to
Llanfairpwllgwyngyllgogerychcchyrndrobwllllantyjiliogogogoch

Day #20 – Lunch on our longest day yet, 17 ½ miles

Day #21 – Windy, rainy, and exposed

Day #21 – Rewards along the way

Day #23 – Hidden cove and crashing waves near Aberderon

Day #24 – Unicorns near Dwyran

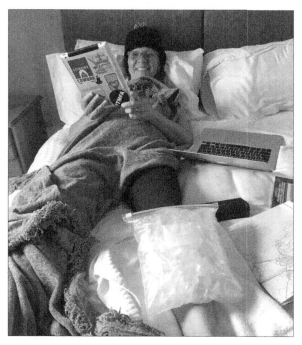

Day #27 – The Shin Split Recovery Unit

Day #29 – The day after Jon was attacked by a cow near Tal-y-Bont

Day #32 - Love

Day #33 – Pointing the way to the iconic Led Zepplin retreat

Day #34 – Leslie finds a friend

Day #35 – Near Aberystwyth

Day #36 – Shit happens

Day #38 – Near Llangrannog

Day #38 – Llangrannog – Our half-way point of the trail

Day #39 – Amazing section of trail near Aberdorth

Day #43 – Journaling at a pub in the village of Pwll Deri

Day #44 – Leslie was afraid of horses before this trip

Day #45 – Blowing 20mph all day long

Day #45 – Rocky cliffs near St. David's

Day #49 – Stone bridge covered by a high tide

Day #51 – Making the most of an all-day rain storm

Day #54 – Village of Tenby

Day #56 – Taking a break in Laugharne

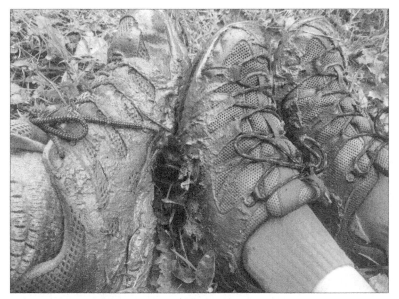

Day #58 – We hope this is mud

Day #59 – Super windy beach hiking near Kidwelly

Day #63 – Some days are better than others

Day #63 – Leslie re-thinking the whole trip on Day 63

Day #63 – Jon re-thinking the whole trip on Day 63

Day #63 – We decide to keep hiking

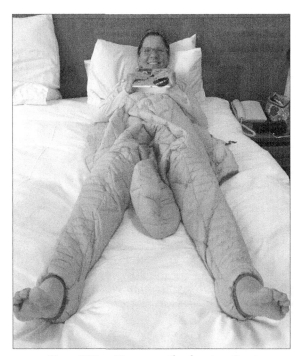

Day #71 – Turn up the heater, Jon!

Day #73 – The end of the Wales Coast Path

Day #73 – Finishing our hike with Monkey Face

Day #73 – Goodbye, stinky hiking shoes!

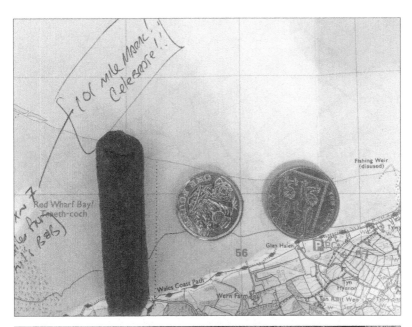

Mileage Milestones

Mileage Milestones

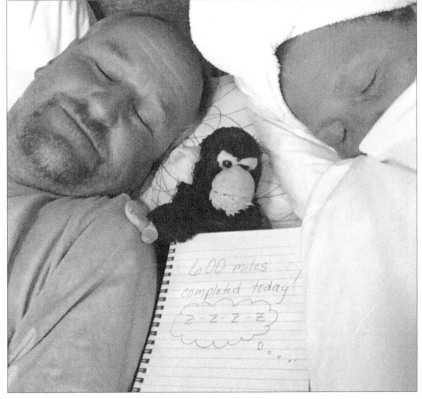

Mileage Milestones

Mileage Milestones

SECTION FOUR: SNOWDONIA & CEREDIGION COAST

Porthmadog to Cardigan

Monday, September 18, 2017, Hiking Day 28
Porthmadog to Harlech
11½ miles; Total – 338 miles

Well, today could've been better. Could have been worse, too, I guess. Leslie's left leg shin splints are bad!! When it's not a dull throbbing ache, it's a sharp shooting pain. We walked from our hotel, the crappy Queen's Hotel, to the Tesco Superstore, maybe 250 yards away, to pick up lunch and snack food, and Leslie was on the verge of tears. She didn't say much, but her teary eyes said it all.

She hobbled on from Tesco a half-mile to the Costa Coffee shop, where we're been all excited about having breakfast this morning, rather than another Welsh breakfast at the hotel. By the time we'd gotten to the coffee shop, she could barely put any weight at all on her left leg. We were both worried that this might be the beginning of the end of our adventure. After icing her shins for hours yesterday evening, and stretching last night and this morning, the pain was worse than ever.

If it's over, it's over. But I'd make sure we at least took two or three days off, with completely no walking, and maybe longer, before we make that decision.

Leslie decided to pop four Advil at once. It was sort of an all or nothing deal. We drank gigantic mugs of good coffee and had muffins, and the I headed to the post office to mail home old maps, the Llyn Peninsula guidebook, Leslie's sandals, and some clothes that we'd replaced with the new stuff we bought on Saturday.

Then I stopped at a pharmacy to buy an ace bandage and ask about what they had for shin splint pain. The pharmacy lady suggested combining Advil with Paracetamol (Tylenol). One for pain and one for inflammation. So, I bought a package of Paracetamol and Leslie downed two more tablets to her pain killer cocktail. And off we hobbled, finally leaving Porthmadog and the Queen's Hotel for good. It was slow going at first, but at least we were moving. Leslie used a hiking pole to take some weight off of her leg and she experimented with various ways to walk, to reduce the strain. Apparently flexing her ankle causes the most pain.

After about 30 minutes the meds kicked in, and the pain mostly went away. It seemed like as long as we were walking on a level walkway or path, she was pretty pain-free. The miracle of over the counter pain meds. Leslie soldiered on and didn't complain one bit. About three miles in we started on a really muddy track through some fields. At one point we turned around, and here comes Nicole up behind us. We ended up walking with her for an hour or so and compared stories about our last four weeks of walking the Wales Coast Path since we'd last seen her. She hasn't met any other through-hikers either. She said that a week or so ago, she too got really bad shin splints, and took one day off. She walked the next day but they were still bad, so she took two more days off, and they got better. So, that's hopeful news.

After about an hour, Nicole went on ahead. She has a lot faster pace than us, especially today. We eventually crossed some very wet muddy fields and then walked along a sloped path of wet grass. At one point Leslie slipped and tweaked her leg, and the sharp pain came right back, so she had to slow way down and was especially careful for fear of slipping again. The grass was wet and there was sheep shit everywhere. Very slippery sheep shit. It was slow going, and Leslie was in pain, but there was no place to go off the trail to allow us to just quit for the day.

We stopped to eat our lunch around 12:30pm, but it immediately started to drizzle so we packed up and kept walking. Around mile eight we hit a little paved road. The sun came out and we sat on a stone bridge rail and ate our lunch of salami, brie, olives, and bread left over from last night's dinner, and sea salt and vinegar chips and tangerines. Leslie took more Advil and Tylenol and off we limped.

We decided to stay on the flat, even road rather than go back to the trail. It was maybe three-quarters of a mile shorter by road, but we had to do it. It was the only way for Leslie to keep her ankle straight, and move forward at all. The final three miles were slow, between Leslie's limping along in pain and the oncoming traffic forcing us off the road at least one hundred times.

We finally made it to Harlech around 3:30pm and met back up with Nicole again, who'd stayed on the trail. She was going to catch a train to Abermouth to the "bunkhouse" where she was staying. We still had another three-quarters of a mile uphill and through town, past the amazing castle in Harlech, to get to our Crown Lodge B&B.

This is by far the nicest place we've stayed yet. The owner put us in the suite because I think we are the only one's here. Two large rooms. An amazing bathroom. The heat is on!!! The towel heating rack works. The shower is hot and powerful and awesome. An amazing room. We are so happy I actually asked if we could stay one more night, thinking I'd encourage Leslie to take tomorrow off, but they are fully booked tomorrow night. Crap.

The two or three restaurants in Harlech are all a half-mile away. So after showers and Leslie's nap, we walked to As Is, a cute little restaurant right at the foot of the castle. Great food. Great wine. And on our way back, we stopped in the Span Market for a chocolate bar for dessert, and the owner of the B&B was there. So, we bought a package of chocolate mints that he recommended, and took him up on his offer to drive us back to the B&B. Perfect way to end the day . . . not having to walk.

Leslie is predicting that her shin splints will be a lot better tomorrow. She put ice on them again tonight, and feels like she has a medication and walking plan that will work. We'll see. . . .

Leslie's Journal Entry:

Tuesday, September 19, 2017, Hiking Day 29
Harlech to Tal-y-bont Train Stop (Lodging in Barmouth at Tal-y-bont B&B)
13 miles; Total – 351 miles

I'm realizing that my journaling has evolved from being a chronological description of the day . . . we had breakfast, we walked to here or there, blah, blah, to what I think were the highlights or the things I remember most about the day.

So, my highlights for today are: old naked men; beer and cider at Ysgethn, a pub at the end or our hike today; a nice relaxing lunch on a beach; and Leslie's shin splints seemed to be improving. I'd add our Skype conversation with Seth and Shauna, but that won't happen until 9:15pm tonight and I won't be journaling after that. So, I'll move that up to first place, ahead of "old naked men." And I'm moving into second place, the place we stayed last night, even though that wasn't on my original list of highlights. It was nothing short of amazing!! Until . . . Mike, the owner of the B&B divulged that Trump and some ultra-conservative politician in the U.K. are his heroes! He literally said "heroes."

He also mentioned that he is against Welsh children doing their schooling in the Welsh language! Even though this is the country of Wales. He boasted, "I'm more Welsh than most people around here, but no one would know it. I've lost accent and don't speak the language." He seemed so proud that he'd given up everything to do with his Welsh heritage. The conversation was a short one. Afterwards, Leslie and I were like, "Did he really say that Trump was his hero?"

Anyway, he and his wife's B&B was fab. Beautiful, large rooms, huge bathroom, kick-ass shower, and a great breakfast this morning. It was also the most expensive place we've stayed. But it was nice. Leslie especially loved the heavy, cozy comforter on the bed. Staying here made us think about the worst places we've stayed on this trip so far: the tiny, crappy Airbnb early on in the trip where we shared the bathroom with several other people who lived there; the Ferry Lodge in Holy Head; and the Queen's Hotel a couple of days ago in Porthmadog.

So, around mile nine today, we got to a huge, beautiful sandy beach that was over two and a half miles long. Enormous. Almost no people. It was a little breezy so we stopped behind a large sand dune and had our lunch. The sun has been out all day today, and it has been beautiful and warm, reminiscent of our first week on the hike. Today was the first really sunny day we've had in a long time (weeks?). With huge, secluded beaches and sunny days, come old naked men flaunting their junk for the world to see. Why? Not sure. But there were 10 or 12 older nude men, some perched up in the dunes; some standing hands on hips surveying the surroundings; others laying on beach towels, with legs spread, big bellies sticking up, and crotches pointing towards to passers-by. And there were the guys walking with their shirts on and pants off. Top half covered, bottom half naked. Why?

One can easily see why this was the highlight of the day.

Leslie was awesome today! She dosed up on meds at breakfast and then again at lunch, and seemed to keep the pain at bay. She was sore and tender at first, but then the meds kicked in. There were a couple of times later in the day when she got some sharp shooting pains, but for the most part she seemed okay. It seems like she's only one misstep away from tweaking it again though.

It was 17 miles from Harlech to Barmouth, and we both knew that was too far to go with Leslie's shin splints, so we stopped at 13 miles, which brought us to the little village of Tal-y-bont. We just missed the train, and the bus wasn't coming for another couple of hours, so we walked a few hundred yards to the Ysgethn Pub and had a drink.

The two taxi companies in Barmouth were busy doing after-school runs for an hour, so we are sitting outside drinking our beer and cider, and appreciating sitting in chairs and not walking.

Tonight, we Skype Seth and Shauna!! Yippee!!

Leslie's Journal Entry:

Wednesday, September 20, 2017, Hiking Day 30
Tal-y-bont Train Stop, through Barmouth to Fairbourne
8 miles; Total – 359 miles

Not the best of days. It is 9:15pm and I don't feel like writing much. We headed out with daypacks this morning, hoping to walk at least 12 miles, backtracking via taxi to the Tal-y-bont train station, on through Barmouth, and then through Fairbourne, and finishing in Llwyngwril.

Things started out fine. We walked the first four and a half miles or so and stopped at a little coffee shop in Barmouth, just a few blocks from our hotel. We saw lots of big black rain clouds zipping over the mountains ahead of us, but everything bad looking seemed to be skirting around us. The weather report was for 50 percent chance of rain beginning at 1pm or 2pm, and then 100 percent by 3pm, with winds starting to pick up.

Neither of us had a lot of energy today. I especially was feeling kind of blah. Leslie's shin splints still hurt, but maybe not quite as bad as the last few days. It always takes a while for the pain meds to kick in.

Out of Barmouth, we walked along an old wooden train bridge, apparently the longest bridge in Wales, like a kilometer long. As we crossed, the wind started picking up, and once we were on the other side, it started to rain. For the next three miles the rain just poured down and the wind drove the rain right into our faces. It was the kind of sideways, driving rain that just ends up penetrating Gortex raincoats. We were both soaked and starting to shiver. There was nowhere to get out of the rain and wind for even a brief few seconds. It was pretty miserable.

The cold rain was just streaming down our faces. I just wasn't physically or mentally prepared for this intense of a rain drubbing. Usually, when I know it is going to rain, I put everything in plastic Ziploc bags including my camera, maps, lunch, guidebook, wallet. Everything gets its own Ziploc. But today I just wasn't prepared.

After about 75 minutes of walking, headlong into this soaking gale, we got into the outskirts of Fairbourne. I stood behind the leeward side of a café that looked closed, just to get out of the wind and rain to check my map. Leslie noticed that the café was open, so we went inside to get something warm to drink, and to regroup.

It was around 12:30pm, so peeled off our wet packs, pack covers, and jackets, and decided to have lunch. A few minutes after sitting down, and watching the wind and rain just thrash the windows, that was showing no sign of stopping, I said, "Well, we could take the train back to Barmouth and just start over again here tomorrow." Leslie was agreeing before I'd even finished my sentence.

So, with only eight miles done today, we called it quits and were both so relieved to be done. Thoughts of a hot shower, dry clothes, and a warm cozy bed took over. We both rationalized (as if rationalizing was needed to take a half-day off after walking for 30 consecutive days) that Leslie's shin splints still needed to heal some more, and we had been thinking of taking a day or two off anyway for them to heal up. So, taking only a half-day off was no big deal. Both of us knew it was the right decision, but it still felt funny to be done walking so soon, and to quit before we'd reached our hiking goal for the day.

I've spent a couple of hours this evening looking at maps and the internet and trying to figure out what to do and how far to go each of these next few days, since we are now off the suggested schedule in the guidebook, and part-way between stops. These next few days (after tomorrow) we head way inland, like 10 miles inland, to go around a river that has no bridge crossing it. And there are not a lot of villages along the way. So, I need to figure things out and then book lodging for the next several nights.

I'm in a bit of a lull, in terms of this hike. It is the middle third of our hike, with still a very long way to go just to get to the half-way point. It's feeling like work and the rain and wind and soaked clothes really take away any fun there might have been. It's the part of a long-distance adventure that most people don't understand. The doing it even when you don't feel like it. When it's not fun.

Leslie's Journal Entry:

Nude beach! Ewwwww.

So, at what point in one's life does this happen? I am genuinely curious. Is it the feeling of freedom? Is it not freeing enough to be naked at home, in private?

We're tired long-distance hikers who like clothes—ON, and who can't help staring. And we really can't. Jon didn't even try to not stare. I tried nonchalantly staring.

Thursday, September 21, 2017, Hiking Day 31
Fairbourne through Llayngwril to Tywyn
(Seabreeze Restaurant and Rooms)
13½ miles; Total – 372½ miles

The highlight of the day was meeting Helen and Simon. About five miles into our day, just after we'd stopped in the little village of Llayngwril to have a snack, we spotted two hikers ahead of us who had just started out for the day.

Helen and Simon are doing day hikes every day for two weeks to complete this section of the Wales Coast Path. They've been section-hiking the Path for the past two years, usually hiking one or two weeks at a time, twice a year. Both were super friendly, ages 38 (Simon) and 41 (not sure how I know that). Simon was amazed at the fact that we were through-hiking the entire trail. He asked several questions about how we handle the mental fatigue of hiking day after day. And how our bodies are holding up.

Simon was a bit self-obsessed, and over the three hours that we hiked together, I heard him tell me about his deep-sea diving experiences; his jobs; his politics (conservative); etc. etc. I barely got a word in edgewise. But the hiking company made the time and the miles fly by. Leslie chatted with Helen the whole way, too. And before we knew it, it was 2:30pm, we hadn't had lunch, and we had only two miles left to finish our 13½-mile day!! So, it was awesome. They were from Nottingham.

The morning portion of the hike was tough. The first hour climbed straight up, out of Fairbourne, on a slippery, muddy track. Rain and mist blew through all morning as we passed a couple of really cool, very old stone farm houses. It was generally a wet and windy first five miles.

We parted ways with our new friends in Tywyn. They were going to walk another mile or so since they'd only gone eight and a half. We called a cab for the four-mile ride to the Seabreeze Restaurant and Rooms. Our taxi driver, Gordon, was awesome. Funny, chatty, and very interested in our adventure. He even drove us through the village of Aberdyfi to point out the evening eating options. We made arrangements with him to pick us up tomorrow and take us back to Tywyn where we left off today.

Our room was on the third floor, which was a killer after a long hike today. I went back out on the street shortly after we arrived, in search of newspaper to stuff in our wet shoes, gallon-sized Ziploc bags (no luck), and alcohol. I ended up buying four gin and tonics in a can, and a bottle of berry flavored hard cider.

So, we sat in our bedroom chairs, looking out of our third-story window onto the sandy beach and ocean that stretched along the length of Aberdyfi just across the street. We had dinner in the restaurant downstairs, and we agreed it was probably the best dinner we've had this entire trip!! Grilled sea bream on veggies and sweet potatoes, awesome fish cakes, and a yummy cauliflower soup, along with some great wine. Really a great dinner. Climbing back up the three flights of stairs took some real effort.

Our Thursday night episode of *Safe House*, episode three, was on tonight, but we both fell asleep by 8:30pm. So, we'll have to find a re-run on the internet to get caught up.

Leslie's Journal Entry:

When it is 8pm and I say I need to take a nap, it means until tomorrow.

We slept through our show.

Walked all day with hikers Helen and Simon. I introduced myself by falling. Falling is so humiliating, no matter what, when it is you, and so damn funny when it is someone else. It's usually me.

Friday, September 22, 2017, Hiking Day 32
Tywyn 4 miles to Aberdyfi and 8 miles to Pennal
(Dyfiview B&B in Machynlleth – Night #1)
12 miles; Total – 384½ miles

Bron-Yr-Aur – An 18th century stone cottage on the outskirts of Machynlleth. The cottage was used in the 1950s by the family of Robert Plant as a holiday home. In 1970, Plant and Jimmy Page spent several months there recuperating after a grueling U.S. Tour. No running water or electricity. They wrote several songs while there including, "Friends", "Bron-Y-Aur Stomp," and "That's The Way." Much of their third album, "Led Zepplin III," was written there.

We've already heard versions of this Led Zepplin story from the first two people we met in Machynlleth this afternoon. We will be walking right past the Bron-Yr-Aur cottage tomorrow morning. Apparently, Robert Plant comes back to the area often, and was just here nine months ago. A guy we met lives in the house right next door. So, I'll take some photos when we walk past tomorrow. I just emailed my brother Steve and brother-in-law Keith about this, since they're both likely to think it's cool that we learned this story.

Today's 12-mile hike would've been way better if it hadn't rained on and off all day. We started by skipping the Welsh breakfast at the Seabreeze. It was an additional £9.50 per person, just for another Welsh breakfast. So, instead we packed up and left. Gordon, our awesome taxi driver picked us up at 8:15am and dropped us off at the co-op grocery in Tywyn just before 9am, where we bought some fresh pasties, milk, cold coffee drinks, and yogurt. We also picked up food for lunch.

We went over to the train station steps and had our breakfast. It was colder than usual this morning, and breezy, so we didn't linger on the steps too long. The four miles back to Aberdyfi took us along the seashore, in and out of bays, and up and down grassy dunes. Leslie's shin splints were really painful this morning and the uneven sandy path wasn't helping. So, we climbed over a barbed-wire fence, and instead walked two miles through a cow pasture, and then the final mile and a half through the middle of a golf course, finishing on a sidewalk that entered the town. After a stop for coffee, the trail followed a narrow road straight up and over a mile-long hill that led back out of town.

We got hit with our first driving rain as we crossed the golf course. I hate getting soaking wet and cold so early in the day, so I was feeling really irritable. Leslie, she just keeps her head down, keeps limping along, without a single complaint. Meanwhile, I'm swearing at the rain, and the trail, and the wind.

For the rest of the day, the trail was way up in the treeless hills. The views were amazing, though a mixture of heavy and light bouts of wind and rain kept blowing through all day. During a brief rain respite, we got down next to a two-foot-high rock wall to get out of the wind, and had our chicken sandwiches and chips, and some really good cherries for lunch.

We'd done a pretty good job of keeping our feet relatively dry, but with a few miles to go, we had to walk through a wet bog, and our feet got completely soaked. At one point, I misjudged a long step and sunk almost up to my knee in water. It was chilly enough that we both put on our new warm winter hats, and Leslie wore my new gloves for the first time. It made me ponder that if we are wearing our winter hats and gloves on September 22nd, what's it going to be like hiking in late October????

By mile 10 or so, the bottoms of my feet usually start to ache and feel tender, so for the last couple of miles we were both limping along. As we got about three-quarters of a mile outside of the village of Pennal, we took refuge from the wind and rain in a little bus shelter, since we were both pretty worn out and soaked.

Once in Pennal, around 3:20pm, I called a local taxi driver, who I could barely understand. He said he had school runs scheduled until after 4:30pm. The only local pub/restaurant was closed until 6pm. So, we sat in another small bus shelter, a bit dispirited. After hiking all day, and being cold and tired, it's a bummer to not be able to get a ride for the final four miles to our B&B. Buses run here every two hours, and we'd missed one by only five minutes, according to the schedule.

After sitting in the little plexiglass bus shelter for 15 minutes or so, a local guy pokes his head in and says, "Are you good hikers?" I said, "I'm not sure if we are good, but we are hikers." Hugh ended up asking if we needed a ride, and loaded us and our wet packs into his car, and drove us to the doorstep of the Dyfiview B&B. So nice. So friendly. Hugh was the first local from Machynlleth to tell us about the Robert Plant and Led Zepplin connection. The kindness of a total stranger. It totally made my day.

Gill and Mike own the Dyfiview B&B. They are older, and avid hikers. Really nice. They immediately took our wet pack covers and soaked socks to hang in the garage and had a dozen "used" balls of newspaper at the door entrance to stuff in our wet shoes. They are a bit anal about enforcing their B&B rules. We had to sign some kind of release form to use their Wi-Fi, in case we ended up using it for illegal purposes. Their "Welcome Guide" in the bedroom has an entire page covering their "Complaint Policy." They both came to our room to show us how to turn on the shower, flush the toilet (no lie), and turn on the TV. Super nice, but very rule conscious.

It felt good to be done for the day. We are here for two nights, so we'll just be hiking with day packs tomorrow. Love that!!

Leslie's Journal Entry:

Am I fermenting? Why do I smell like vinegar?

Saturday, September 23, 2017, Hiking Day 33
Pennal through Machynlleth to Furnace Bridge
(Dyfiview B&B in Machynlleth – Night #2)
11 miles; Total – 395½ miles

I was up at my usual 6:45am to journal, check internet news and the weather, and get a little work done. Breakfast at 8:15am was great. It's so cute that Gill and Mike are side-by-side seemingly every second. They greeted us together this morning, took our breakfast order together, served the food together, and literally stood right next to each other the whole time we ate and chatted.

Leslie noticed that they offer to make a hiker's lunch, so we requested lunches for tomorrow. The dining room and "lounge" has lots of hiking information and maps and related stuff. I saw two books on display for sale and realized that they were both written by Mike! One book was the chronicle of their hike of the Coast-to-Coast Path across England about 10 years ago. The second book is about their travels in Egypt. The book cover says that it is full of funny stories, and written in the style of Bill Bryson. The books are available on Amazon so I'll buy them when I get home.

Our taxi lady this morning, from "Pete's Taxi," came right at 9am, and we were back in Pennal to start walking a few minutes later. As soon as I got out of the taxi, I realized I'd forgotten my phone, which is also my camera. We are only hiking with day packs today, so we left most of our stuff at the B&B . . . and also my phone, apparently. I was super annoyed and bummed, until I realized that after four miles of hiking, we walked right back into Machynlleth and only a few blocks from our B&B. The only bummer was that this morning was when we walked past Bron-Yr-Aur and I'd promised photos of the Led Zepplin cottage for Steve and Keith. So, all day, I knew I'd be heading back out after our hike to get some photos, even though it'll involve lots more walking. It'll be my little pilgrimage for my brother and brother-in-law.

It turned out to be a beautiful hiking day. Our first day with zero rain in a while. Cloudy and muggy, but with a breeze in the morning. The sun was out for most of the afternoon and the temp hit 68 degrees. The entire day the trail was up in the mountains, and there was a lot of forest walking through huge towering pine trees. It reminded me of Southeast Alaska with ferns on the ground and huge coniferous trees all around. It was really quiet and peaceful. No wind, no ocean, no cars, and no people. And really different from any hiking we've done so far on the WCP because we are so far inland now.

The day basically consisted of four major uphills, each taking 30 to 60 minutes, and then four major downhills that took a fraction of the time. Lots of good exercise and hopefully we burned some calories over the 11 miles. Leslie's shin splints were okay when medicated, but once again by the end of the day, the last few miles were pretty slow and painful.

We called our taxi lady from Furnace Bridge in the little abandoned village of Furnace that had once been (in the 1800s) the location of a huge coal-fired smelting furnace that now lies in ruins. The taxi dropped Leslie off at our B&B around 3:45pm and then drove me back to the base of the narrow road that led up to Bron-Yr-Aur. The taxi wouldn't head up the road because it was so steep and narrow.

I'd already had been walking for six and a half hours but didn't want to pass up the chance of taking a few photos for Steve and Keith. The one-car-wide lane climbed steeply up the mountainside for about half a mile to a narrower drive that had "Bron-Yr-Aur" painted in white on a big stone. Next to the stone was a little fruit and vegetable stand where one could buy apples and little home-made purses by leaving money in an envelope.

On up the narrow driveway I walked, expecting to see the house around every corner. I was a little nervous because we'd heard from a few local people that the folks who now own the cottage don't appreciate visitors. Many Led Zepplin fans make the pilgrimage to the site that is credited for really launching the band into infamy.

After about another half a mile, I met a mom, dad, and young daughter on the roadside, checking out some erosion that was eating at part of the road. They turned out to be the owners of the cottage. Scott and Ruth(?) were initially a bit cold and mildly annoyed when I said I was looking for the Led Zepplin house. I instantly felt bad, like I was encroaching on their privacy, even though we were on a public lane. So, I just stopped walking and started up a conversation that ended up lasting two hours, and covering everything from controlling erosion, to Donald Trump;s idiocy, to U.K. politics, Welsh/Brit relations, the importance of being bilingual, and immigration, to name a few of the topics we hit on.

They were super interesting and very cool people. Ruth was a schoolteacher, and Scott was an Ecologist. After we'd built some rapport, and I'd explained that truthfully, I didn't give a shit about Led Zepplin and that I was only getting photos for my brother and brother-in-law, they invited me to walk back to the house with them, and through the gate into their yard.

They have made the commitment to live off the grid as much as possible, so through a combination of solar panels, a small wind turbine, and hydropower from the creek, they generate all of their own electricity. They've lived here for six years and are experimenting with all kinds of vegetable and fruit growing techniques on the small half-acre they own. Their efforts include hydroponics, and growing root vegetables in bales of hay. They are successfully growing grapes for wine in an area of Wales where grapes just don't grow. And they are successfully growing hops for beer, again, in an area where hops aren't supposed to grow. We also talked about the Haida people that I work for, and the idea of doing some kind of cultural exchange, and so we shared email addresses before I left.

They said that they'd love to be able to welcome every visitor that comes, but sometimes they come by the dozens, and often daily, and it's just too much. And apparently, over the years, people have exploited their friendliness and so they've become more cautious and rarely invite anyone into their yard. Towards the end of our awesome conversation, they asked if I wanted to come inside for coffee or tea.

They have poor to non-existent cell service, so after about an hour, I saw a text from Leslie wondering if I'd been shot or abducted. So, I texted her right back, and a half-hour later realized that my text never went through. So, I knew that I needed to get going.

Scott and Ruth believe that the cottage and surrounding area have an almost mystical way of fostering creativity and inspiration. They have hosted a few artists, writers, and musicians over the years, and a few musician retreats. They shared several stories of cool experiences they've had, and cool people they've met here at Bron-Yr-Aur over the past six years.

I really appreciated meeting them, and especially inviting me in for coffee. I hope to stay connected in some way. They were especially interested in the projects going on in Hydaburg, Alaska, where I work. So, maybe there's some kind of connection there.

It was a long walk back to town. Maybe a mile and a half, and I'd been standing or walking pretty much since 9am. I got back to town a bit after 6pm. I met Leslie in town at the Taj Mahal Indian restaurant for dinner. A great and very cool day!!

Leslie's Journal Entry:

I have determined that our cute little B&B host and hostess are actually Siamese twins as I have yet to see them separate from each other.

Sunday, September 24, 2017, Hiking Day 34
Furnace Bridge to Borth (Aberystwyth Bellevue Royal Hotel)
8 miles; Total – 403½ miles

The most memorable parts of today's walk were the mud and the horses. We were all packed up at our Dyfiview B&B by 8:15am and had our millionth Welsh breakfast. Leslie has been switching off between having a cold breakfast of granola or muesli with yogurt and fruit, toast and jam, alternating with eggs, bacon, toast, and the rest of the traditional Welsh breakfast. I've gone from the "Full Welsh" to asking for just two eggs, toast, and bacon. And I usually start with a bowl of Special-K or Corn Flakes, and always have orange juice. So, after 33 days of eating the same breakfast, I'm passing on the baked beans, fried tomato, and occasional hash brown triangle, or fried toast the comes with the Full Welsh.

Anyway, since it seems like I've barely lost a pound over the last 400 miles, I'm going to try to have occasional cold breakfasts too . . . maybe a little less daily bacon will help. If I also focus on no sugary drinks and little or no fried food for dinner, maybe I'll see some progress on my waistline. It seems common sense that since we are walking all day long, I should be able to eat whatever I want. But since my goal is to also lose some weight, I need to make a few changes in my hiking diet.

We had a short day by design today. Only eight miles. Tomorrow is even shorter. But it's coming at a good time since Leslie's shin splints aren't getting any better, which is a big concern. She also hasn't been doing a good job of icing her shins at the end of the day. But we'll be able to give them a bit of a break today and tomorrow.

So, the mud and horses. The first four miles took us up into the hills out of Furnace, through several pastures, and across a few creeks. It reminded me of hiking in the woods of Southern Indiana, which we rarely do. I can see that fall is on its way as well. Almost all of the ferns are brown and dead now, which gives the hillsides a reddish-brown hue.

Around mile four, we dropped own into the village of Tre'r-ddol. There was a flea market on a grassy field that was signed, "Outdoor Market and Boot Sale." I eventually realized that "boot" meant the trunk of a car. We stopped in a cute little coffee shop that was run by a non-profit, and sold locally sourced stuff, and was run by volunteers. We passed a big old church with an overgrown churchyard that was for sale. I looked it up online later and it was £139,000, or about $180,000US. Super cool. Partly renovated. It would make a great pub, coffee shop, bakery, or all of the above.

Anyway, the next four miles were flat but super swampy and muddy. Lot of standing water and deep mud mixed with cow shit as the trail led through several cow pastures. Super irritating. The poopy mud almost pulled my shoes off several times. And Leslie hates wet feet and muddy shoes, so we were both grumbling.

We stopped for lunch on the wooden steps of a little foot bridge. Gnats biting. Feet soaked and smelly. Slight drizzle. Not very fun. But the highlight? We saw several horses along the way. We stopped to feed one some fresh grass, and I fed a few others my apple from lunch. At one point, Leslie said, "I guess I like horses now." Apparently, she's never really liked them before.

Leslie's Journal Entry:

I don't know what it is but walking in ankle-deep mud is just not fun. Eating lunch in the rain is not that much fun either, really.

But . . . I have decided I like horses now. I have not liked them since a birthday party I went to in the second grade. I got there late, and all the little cute ponies were taken so I was given a huge adult-sized horse who liked to gallop and terrorize seven-year-olds. They've scared me for 45 years. But, I am over it now!

Monday, September 25, 2017, Hiking Day 35
Borth to Aberystwuth (2nd Nite in Aberystwyth)
6¼ miles; Total – 409¾ miles

Yesterday's journal entry ended a little abruptly.

Aberystwyth is a Victorian seaside city like ones we saw and stayed at on the north coast of Wales at the beginning of this hike. It was gray and rainy when we got here yesterday afternoon. So, not many people were walking around. But today, the sun came out this afternoon and there are lots of people milling around the promenade. There is also a university here with 12,000 students, and they just came back last week. So, lots of young people, and plenty of restaurants. It's definitely one of the largest towns we've walked through so far.

Last night we were hoping to go to a Caribbean restaurant, Momma Feys, but it was closed unexpectedly. So, we ended up at more of a pub-like place. Tonight, we both want to find something better for dinner.

The trail guidebook that we are following shows only six and a quarter miles today. We were originally thinking of adding three or four miles to make tomorrow's 13-mile hike easier, but instead, we decided to just stick with six miles and treat it like a day off. Maybe 8 miles yesterday, and only 6 miles today, with a big bag of ice for Leslie's shins on both days, will start to heal things up.

It felt weird actually. We started walking out of Borth around 9:15am and were done and walking back into our hotel, the Bellevue Royal, around 11:45am!! So, rather than think that we didn't go very far, I'm thinking that we got six miles done on a day off! A mind game, I know. But so much of this hike is a mind game to keep going day after day after day.

The hike was beautiful. We walked in and out of morning fog. But it was great to be back on the coast after three days away. The trail was high up on sheer cliffs and we had the sound of crashing waves and squawking seagulls to remind us that were back on the coast. There were a few decent ascents and descents, so hopefully we burned a few calories.

The afternoon has been relaxing. I rested for a couple of hours in the room and then went to a post office to mail home three maps; got a much-needed haircut; went to an ATM; got a good coffee; and have been sitting in the hotel lounge for the past two or three hours catching up on work, reviewing our upcoming hiking route for the next few days, and journaling while Leslie relaxes upstairs in our room. It feels good to get caught up on things.

I also stopped in a camping store and bought a super lightweight down jacket. Extra weight to carry, but as it gets cooler in October, it'll be nice to have. And it was only £50, regularly £150! Couldn't pass it up.

At about 1:00am this morning I woke up to check the Packers vs. Bengals score. The Packers won after a late fourth quarter touchdown drive and a field goal in overtime. Nice.

We're going to Skype with Seth and Shauna tonight. So that'll be fun. It's around 5pm so we'll get some dinner and maybe a drink at the hotel, and then do our best to stay awake until 9:15pm when we arranged to Skype.

Tomorrow the route has lots of ups and downs and is 13 miles, so we'll start a little earlier than usual and are both just getting our minds ready for a strenuous day.

Leslie's Journal Entry:

Jon is trying to guilt me into writing in my journal more. Today he said I didn't have to write in it, but that it "would ruin everything."

Well, not wanting to be a ruiner, I am writing today, even though it is our day off (we walked five miles but are calling it a day off).

Jon is mean.

Tuesday, September 26, 2017, Hiking Day 36
Aberystwyth to Llanon
13¼ miles; Total – 423 miles

The highlight of the day was finally being able to Skype with Seth. Shauna had school meetings, so she wasn't home. But this is the third time we've scheduled a Skype call. The first two times we had crappy internet and had to cancel. Seth showed us around his yard in Houghton, Michigan . . . newly painted deck rails, remodeled bar in his extended garage, new trench and drainage pipe. Lots of projects. He was getting ready to go out with his buddy Nolan to set up a deer blind for hunting season that's about to begin. It was great to see him and catch up a bit. I'm hoping to get up to Michigan sometime after Thanksgiving.

Today was a long hike with full packs. Walking out of our hotel in Aberystwyth this morning my pack was the heaviest it has been since we started. Lots of food, my new down jacket, two books, four maps. I've just been accumulating things and today I noticed the extra weight. Altogether, my pack is still probably less than 35 pounds. And Leslie's, I'm sure, has creeped above 30 pounds. We are both carrying medium-sized packs and they are completely stuffed full.

Today was probably the most "remote" section of the Wales Coast Path so far, to the extent that anything in the small country of Wales is remote. For the entire 13 miles we didn't see anyone else on the trail, and didn't pass over any roads or go through any villages. So, it felt more isolated than usual. The trail stayed high up on a cliff, sometimes running just a few feet from the sheer drops of several hundred feet.

Leslie's courage and fear of heights has definitely improved over these two long backpacking trips. She doesn't bat an eye anymore when she walks along these steep and dangerous drop-offs. It was a beautiful day of hiking, but hard work. We started out a few minutes after 8am and didn't get to Llanon and our Prysg B&B until after 4pm.

A couple of times we walked near big, very old stone houses that had tumbled down and fallen into rocky disarray, but both were being rebuilt by someone. Both houses were in really remote locations along the sea. One looked like the building efforts and scaffolding had been abandoned. Maybe someone ran out of money. Seeing these remote stone houses got me fantasizing about buying an old fallen-down stone house and completely rebuilding it. I've mentioned it to Leslie so many times, and she just laughs. But the remote location, the challenge of rebuilding, the stunning scenery, the peace and quiet. And maybe creating a hiker's B&B or an artist's and writer's retreat all appeal to me. I do need a home remodel or project.

The weather was great. Overcast and cool, but no rain. Just another long and strenuous hiking day in a place that I'm trying hard not to take for granted. Tonight, at Prsyg B&B, we did two much-needed loads of laundry and hung our wet stuff out on an outside clothes line, and inside on heaters. What a luxury to have a washer and be able to wash all of our clothes!!

Leslie's Journal Entry:

Five weeks on the trail today. Five and a half to six weeks to go. I am having a great time and feel strong but can't decide if I'm excited or depressed about how much we still have to go.

Hmmm . . . should have read the fine print on our Airbnb listing that said to "bring your own towels" before I jumped in the shower.

Wednesday, September 27, 2017, Hiking Day 37
Llanon to New Quay
11½ miles; Total – 434½ miles

We had a good hiking day today. At one point, Leslie said that this was the best she's felt in the past 10 days. Her left shin splints are way better, and she walked the entire day without a headache. Also, there was no rain to speak of until right around when we finished our hike at 1:45pm. There was a bit of a breeze all day, but the wind didn't pick up until we were almost done walking, and then it really picked up. t was overcast all day with temperatures around 60 degrees. And, best of all, we hiked with just a daypack, leaving our stuff in Llanon at the Prysg Villa Airbnb. So, from all measures, including the fact that it was a very manageable mileage day of 11½ miles, it was a great day!

It was so fun this morning to wake up, come downstairs to the kitchen and make fresh coffee in a coffee press. We've actually had pressed coffee at several B&Bs and hotels, but they use such a little bit of coffee that it always tastes like water. Even the Starbucks coffee I got in Aberystwyth before we left town was watery. Big disappointment. Anyway, I made our own coffee, and had breakfast sitting on the couch in the living room. It was just nice being in more like a house, rather than a room. We sat around for a while, and then literally walked right out our back door, and down a quarter-mile trail to link up with the WCP. Super convenient.

The first couple of miles heading towards Aberarth were flat. Then there were a few miles of ups and then dropping down into small creek valleys, and back up again. But there were only a few short muddy spots, so the hiking was really enjoyable. The sea has been calm over the past few days. Almost placid like a lake.

It is definitely starting to feel like fall. All of the ferns are dead and brown, the trailside blackberries are all shriveled or gone. We even walked through a couple of short broadleaf forest sections where the trail was covered in fallen leaves. Back home in the Midwest it has been in the 90s. But here it feels like fall.

At about five and a half miles, we walked into Aberarth, a cute little seaside village where the houses that lined the harbor were all painted bright colors. It reminded me of the brightly colored buildings lining the river entrance to Willemstad, Curacao. The next six miles were just as pleasant. My right knee and right hip and groin were stiff and achy today, but I took three Advil and it felt a lot better. My left knee has been sort of buckling a few times a day recently, too. Maybe five or six times a day I'll over-extend my step, or twist my knee slightly, and I'll get a sharp shooting pain in the top of my kneecap. I remember this happening on the Southwest Coast Path, too. Using my hiking poles, I have to favor that side until the pain goes away.

After a late lunch at the Black Lion pub in New Quay, we got a taxi back to Llanon. Our big treat tonight was not only making our own dinner in our very own kitchen, but Leslie figured out how to watch back episodes of BBC shows, so we watched the third episode of *Safe House* while eating ice cream! Just in time, because the fourth episode is on tomorrow night at 9pm.

Leslie's Journal Entry:

Toward the end of our walk, it started to sprinkle and the wind picked up so I zipped up my raincoat and put up my hood. When Jon turned around, he said, "Whoa! Someone is really battening down the hatches." He makes me laugh.

Thursday, September 28, 2017, Hiking Day 38
New Quay to Llangrannog (8½) to Penbryn (2½)
11 miles; Total – 445½ miles

We hit our halfway point today!! So far, we've ended up hiking about 10 extra miles somehow (getting to our lodging mostly), so the overall trail length of 870 miles becomes 880 miles, and we got to our 440-mile mark today around noon. It's also hiking day 38 today, and we've been estimating that the overall hike will take 75 or 76 days. In some ways, I've been anticipating this day for a long time. When we'd only been hiking for 10 days, or 20 days, getting to the halfway point seemed like a major goal. Every mile and day after this point somehow now seems to get us closer to our overall goal than the miles we walked in the first half. It's not that I'm wishing it to be over, but during an extended adventure like this, reaching smaller goals and milestones help keep up my morale and motivation.

Yesterday, Leslie said something like, "It seems so weird sometimes to think that we are doing this. Hiking 870 miles. It just hits me sometimes. Like what the heck are we doing? Why are we doing this?" I don't think that either of us really thinks about the "why" very often. We just get up and go every single day. I we want to finish, then we just have to get up and go. There isn't really any room to get up in the morning and say, "We don't want to go today." Of course, we could do that a few times, here and there, but it's a slippery slope to start thinking that way. "Oh, let's not go today because it's raining so hard," or "It's too windy," or "My knees ache too much." I could think of an excuse almost every single day to not hike. Also, neither of us want to be doing this hike into mid-November. We actually do have work and other commitments and priorities back home, and pets, and a house, and a business, etc.

People have asked us a few times why we are doing this and at those times I realize that I don't have a very good or consistent answer. I'm not certain on any given day myself. And maybe the reasons aren't all conscious or clear. Or maybe words can't describe the reasons, and it is more of a feeling. We are both goal oriented when it comes to this trip and completing the entire 870 miles in one go. And we both are motivated by the physical challenge. Can we do this at our age? But the goal and the challenge doesn't sustain either of us on a day-to-day, hour-to-hour basis. The scenery, the culture, the people who we meet. These are the things I'll remember the most, and that provides the short-term motivation.

Yesterday, we met a couple about our age, coming towards us. They were on a day hike, and we stopped to chat for a few minutes. They live near Chepstow where we'll finish our hike, and they were so amazed and impressed with what we were doing. Finally, the lady said, "Well, you better get going. You still have a long way to go." And the guy said, "Congratulations on reaching your half-way mark." And to be honest, I got a little choked up hearing him say that. That was the sum total of our "congratulations" at the moment we'd hiked 440 miles. A stranger just saying, "Good job. Congratulations." So, that's part of it, too. Feeling a sense of accomplishment. And hearing someone else acknowledge our accomplishment.

We have a great cheering section back home, too. I've been sending photos out every couple of days to family, and we always get two or three responses, usually from or parents and from Seth. They are the ones who respond with a supportive comment pretty much every time I send photos or a brief update.

After we passed the hiking couple, we stopped to record a short "half-way video" on the trail. It was like a minute long. We sent it out to our family group. Hopefully, everyone can figure out how to open and view the file.

Today turned out to probably be our hardest hiking day to date. It was only 11 miles, but non-stop up and down steep trails. A lot of the steep sections either had steps built, or muddy little ledges dug into the hillside for each step. It was slow going, and both our sets of knees were really aching for most of the day, despite regular dosing of Advil. We traveled on a remote section of trail with some of the most stunning scenery that we've experienced. Little secluded bays and high cliffs overlooking the ocean. The sun was out pretty much all day long. Just a beautiful day with a light breeze. A perfect hiking day.

At around mile 10 out of New Quay, we dropped down into the tiny picturesque village of Llangrannog, and a beach full of school children on a field trip, with many lined up to buy ice cream. It was a weird switch after hiking for five hours through a pretty remote section of trail. We stopped and got some lunch, trying to look and act like normal tourists, but probably not blending in with our dirty backpacks, muddy shoes, and grungy clothes.

The final two and a half miles were basically a mile and a quarter straight uphill, and then a mile and a quarter back down to a spot called Penbryn, which is a National Trust area with a small beach.

There is nothing at Penbryn except a couple of really old stone buildings and a coffee shop called The Plump Tart that we'd hoped would be open, but was closed "due to family circumstances."

So, we sat at a picnic table and barely got a cell signal out to call a taxi, who didn't show up for another hour. We sat and read our books. I took off my wet shoes and wet socks to air out my feet a little. The taxi came a little earlier than expected and it was the same driver who had taken us from New Quay back to Llanon the other day. It was fun to see a familiar face and update him on our journey as he drove us to Cardigan, and the most amazing B&B yet!

Leslie's Journal Entry:

Seriously, like where are we again? I am starting to lose track. All this walking and eating in pubs and sleeping in white cozy comforters has me confused. I know we are NOT home, because there is only one kind of salad dressing here.

Friday, September 29, 2017, Hiking Day 39
Penbryn to Aberdorth (3¼ miles) to Gwbert Hotel (9 miles)
Stayed at Quay 23 Loft B&B – Amazing
12¼ miles; Total – 457¾ miles

Today was a good hiking day for a few reasons. There were three noteworthy stops or things to look forward to along the way, which always helps make the miles go by more quickly; the weather was great with some sun, some clouds, some light breeze, and a bout of rain towards the end; and there were several climbs and descents, but not as long or as steep and severe as yesterday; and the last three miles were the easiest and the flattest which is always a great way to end a 12½-mile hike with full backpacks.

We caught a taxi to Penbryn, the little closed café where we ended up yesterday. There was a cool unoccupied stone house next door. Not for sale or anything, but every time I see a cool old stone house that looks abandoned, or empty, or for sale, I daydream about buying it and fixing it up.

Two miles into the hike we walked through a cute little village— Treath, or something like that. Even though we'd only walked a couple of miles, we were both starving after the breakfast we made for ourselves of yogurt and cereal. So, we gorged on some snacks and then walked another mile and a half into Aberporth. We'd planned on finding a grocery store here to buy food for lunch. The trail, of course, led along the shore and passed a little café. I popped in and asked about the nearest store, which was a 10-minute walk out of the way, so instead we bought a meat pastie, a beef pie, and two cans of soda, and loaded them in our packs for lunch.

The route followed a road that climbed steeply out of Aberporth, and then wound around a military base and a firing range. Although it didn't rain for most of the day, the trail was really muddy and slippery, and the high grass was soaked from overnight rain and dew, so it was another day of walking in soaked socks and shoes. Today, my right sock must have been bunched up around my little toe, because I developed my first blister of the trip.

We were pushing for around the nine-mile point to stop for lunch. It was a 12th century church—Mwnch. A thick-walled, whitewashed stone chapel that had a baptismal font from the 1100s and pieces of carved wood depicting the heads and faces of the twelve disciples dating back 700 or 800 years. Pretty wild. We read that people in this Mwnch Valley were known to be really hearty back a few hundred years ago, and were referred to as the "Giants of Mwnch." Many lived to be over 100 years old, which in the 1700s and 1800s was pretty damn old. There was an old cemetery next to the church that did indeed show a few 100-plus-year-olders.

As we settled down on the steps of the ancient stone church to dig our lunch food out of our packs, it started pouring down rain, so we brought our pastie, meat pie, and sodas and chips into the last row of pews and had our lunch in the little church. It felt a little sacriligous, but the church was providing comfort to the hungry and weary, so we figured it was okay. We just kicked the pastie crumbs underneath the pew before we left.

Our B&B was in Cardigan, a really cute larger town with lots of shops and cafés, and the Cardigan Castle, which looked pretty touristy. The room we stayed in was a third-floor attic, converted into an amazing loft apartment, with skylights, ancient original wood beams in the ceiling, and a little well-equipped kitchenette. Definitely the coolest place we've stayed in yet, 23 Quay Street. It was warm and cozy, with chairs and a couch. Everything we needed to cook dinner. We planned to stay for two nights, so it was perfect.

I went off to find a store to buy dinner stuff, including pork chops, potatoes, wine, and breakfast food from a little bakery that had amazing muffins and desserts, and a loaf of bread. It felt like we were on vacation.

We settled in and didn't budge for the rest of the night. Good internet. Cozy chairs. Great bed. The perfect place to spend two nights. Maybe we won't leave.

Leslie's Journal Entry:

Sometimes when taking selfies, Jon and I fight over who has to put their head more forward so one head doesn't look huger than the other. We take turns.

Saturday, September 30, 2017, Hiking Day 40
Gwbert Hotel to Cardigan (3½ miles) to Poppit Beach Youth Hostel (3½ miles)
7 miles; Total – 464¾ miles

Today was sort of a weird "day off," even though we ended up walking about seven miles. The next section of the Wales Coast Path is the first stage of our "Guidebook #5: Pembrokshire" and this next 17 miles is supposed to be the most difficult section of the entire coastal path. So, we still had three and a half miles to walk this morning from where we stopped yesterday to get into Cardigan, and then decided to hike the first three and a half miles of the 17-mile day, to a youth hostel. We would have loved to catch a ride back to spend a third night in the loft, but it wasn't available. So, youth hostel it will be.

With not much hiking to do on this very rainy and miserable day, we stayed in our loft until 10am, just enjoying the morning. We met the owner, Penny, on our way out the door, and then caught a taxi to Gwbert Hotel and quickly walked the three and a half miles back to Cardigan in a steady rain.

Then we proceeded to basically kill the next three hours in town, since the hostel didn't open until 5pm, so it didn't make any sense to hike there in the rain, and then sit outside for a few hours. We had a "comfort food" lunch of roast beef, potatoes, and veggies at a little café. We then walked to a coffee shop and settled in for a couple of hours to read and drink coffee while the rain continued to pour down. We were both chilled and wet.

Around 3pm we grabbed our packs, now heavier with dinner for tonight and tomorrow's breakfast and lunch, since the hostel is out of town and not near any place to buy food. Plus, we still had some beer and whiskey and lemon juice that we are also carrying. So, we stuffed our packs as full as we could, and I carried a grocery bag full of food, in the drizzle, for the three and a half miles to the hostel.

Paul, the volunteer hostel host, let us in a little early and we set-tled into our tiny room. No ensuite bathroom. The room reminded me of a small berth on a ship. And the little public shower room reminded me, too, of the shower rooms on the Alaska Marine Line ferries.

Right now, we're sitting in the hostel lounge. I'm journaling and Leslie is playing candy crush on her iPad, and doing a little read-ing. We'll make our dinner of grilled cheese and instant soup, have a couple of drinks, and then probably head to our little room for the night. There are nine people here at the hostel tonight. A group of three men, a single guy, a single young woman, another cou-ple, and us. The kitchen looks great. It's a nice hostel with an awe-some ocean view. But hostels aren't really our thing. Especially the shared showers and bathrooms.

Tomorrow is a big day!!

Leslie's Journal Entry:

For the last two nights we have been in an adorable loft apartment with tasteful furnishings, old wooden rafters, and cozy pillows and comforters.

Tonight, we are at a youth hostel. Basically, an Ikea without the tasty meatballs. That's all I'm saying.

SECTION FIVE: PEMBROKESHIRE

Cardigan to Amroth

Sunday, October 1, 2017, Hiking Day 41
Poppit Beach Youth Hostel to Newport
12¼ miles; Total – 477 miles

October!

Seems like a milestone worth celebrating.

We hiked through the last week of August, and through all of September. The whole damn month!

And now it's October.

Once we get to the end of October, we'll be running to finish the last few days!!

Since the weather has been so unseasonably rainy and cold in September (as we've been told many times), my optimistic theory is that October will be unseasonably sunny and warm!

Well . . . today was not the October I was hoping for. Maybe it is still getting the September weather out of its system? Because today's weather sucked!! It was rainy and windy and chilly all day long. And it was that fine misty rain that sticks to your eyebrows and face.

The first two or three miles we could see rain coming towards us from across the water, so we'd put our raincoats on, and then it would just be a light mist and I'd get all sweaty and stop again to take my raincoat off a few minutes later.

At one point, we came up onto a rocky rise and got hit by a blast of wind. The weather report said winds at 20mph pretty much all day, with gusts to 40mph. So, we stopped to put on raincoats again, and Leslie put her rain pants on. It was so windy that we had a hard time getting our stuff on. I shot a short video of the wind and of Leslie trying to get her rain pants on. The strong wind didn't last long, but it reminded us of days a few weeks ago when we got hammered by the wind.

The trail was pretty wet and muddy. And with the rain and the wind, we decided about halfway through the day to take a road route instead. The muddy trail was super slippery and I was sliding all over. And we were both starting to feel a bit chilled by the wind and rain. The road route cut off about a mile, but it was the right choice given the circumstances.

We got to Newport Sands, a big sandy beach just after 1pm, and sat behind a closed lifeguard building to get out of the wind. The picnic table behind the building was wet and we were both pretty chilled, but at least we had a spot out of the wind to eat our lunch.

This morning I made peanut butter and jelly sandwiches in the hostel kitchen before Leslie got up. They tasted great for lunch today, along with sea salt and vinegar chips and some generic Ho Hos that we got at the Spare market yesterday. The cold and soaking rain made my knee and ankle joints feel especially achy the last few miles. I spent a lot of time thinking about the hot tub I want to buy and install when we get home. And how nice it would be to be soaking in one right now.

The B&B we are at tonight in Newport is called the Cnapan, and is wonderful. Mike and Judy met us at the door. It's a cool, very old stone house with five B&B bedrooms. Their family has been operating the Cnapan for three generations. Great shower, cozy bed, and Mike offered to do a load of laundry for us. Jackpot!!

We just finished dinner at a local pizza place that had great pizza and a goat cheese, walnut, and rocket salad. And local beer. It was run by some young people who were super friendly and gave off a great vibe.

Tomorrow the weather is supposed to be better. It is only 8:30pm, but I think we'll be out by 9pm. I think the hiking and ups and downs of the trail day after day are starting to wear on my knees and ankles. I noticed my left ankle was especially stiff and sore today. I don't think we're getting in any better shape after 40 days of hiking. As a matter of fact, it almost feels like the opposite. That we are wearing our bodies down a bit. I feel it especially first thing in the morning. Everything aches until I get moving. I don't remember these aches and pains 10 to 20 years ago.

I wore my new lightweight down jacket to dinner tonight. I love it. Fall is in the air.

Leslie's Journal Entry:

After losing my third round of *Guess What Color the Next Car is Going to Be*, I said, "What if I start losing at *Yahtzee*, too?"

Jon: *You're gonna need to talk to your therapist about that.*

Monday, October 2, 2017, Hiking Day 42
Newport to Fish Guard
10 miles; Total – 487 miles

"Best sandwiches ever!" or "Mud, mud, mud." Where do I begin?

Let's start with the sandwiches.

So much of our trip is focused on food. Thinking and talking about what we'll eat for dinner is a daily obsession, and often is all that gets us through the day. Planning varied breakfasts is a challenge given the choices at B&Bs and what's available at the local Tesco when we are eating on our own. Lunch gives us a little opportunity to exercise some creativity, but again, the little 7-Eleven-type Tesco and Spars and Premiers don't offer much variety. This morning, before breakfast, I walked to the Spar to pick up lunch stuff and ended up with some fresh baked and still warm whole wheat bap buns, some smoked ham, and processed cheese slices, and a giant container of mayo that we'll only use a fraction of.

When I got back to the room, I made two deluxe smoked ham, processed cheese, and mayo sandwiches that turned out to be incredible; and an awesome peanut butter and jelly sandwich for Leslie that was equally to-die-for. We stopped for lunch today, mid-walk, and sat in a little sheltered area on stone benches that a family built to honor of their 22-year-old son, Henry, who died while in the military only a few years ago. We ate our big tasty sandwiches and thanked Henry and his family for building this little sanctuary out of the wind, where we could sit and enjoy our lunch!!

About 95 percent of the trail today was muddy, way more than yesterday. Virtually every step was in slippery, wet mud. Not very deep, but constant. And since there were no level parts of the trail today, every step had to be carefully placed. And we had to take small steps, too, to decrease the chance of slipping. So, it was slow going and tedious walking all day long. This is where my two hiking poles came in extra handy. I hike all day, every day with two adjustable hiking poles, and I was happy to have them today.

We only went 11 miles, the last mile of which was on a sidewalk, but the 10 muddy miles took almost six hours to negotiate. And as Leslie said a couple of times during the day, we spent all day looking at our feet and rarely looked up and around at the beautiful scenery.

Leslie started the morning with a bad headache, and then having to concentrate so much on balancing and not slipping made it worse as the day wore on. We both slipped and slid scores of times during the day, but once, Leslie completely fell over into a bank of stinging nettles that brushed against her arm and face, and stung for the rest of the day. But in true fashionista style, she did not get a single bit of mud on her jacket or her pants when she fell. Well done, Leslie.

Last week I was in a bit of a slump emotionally, with the thought of how far we still had to go on this hike. But today it was Leslie's turn. A few times she lamented that we still have about 35 days of walking to go. And the combination of the mud, her headaches, and the worse-than-predicted weather today all contributed to Leslie feeling a bit blue about the whole adventure.

As we neared the town of Fish Guard, we passed the remnants of an old stone fort on a hill. Several hundred years old, that still had four big cannons pointing out into the sea. So, I climbed onto one of the cannons for my obligatory photo of a Wunrow boy sitting on a canon. My dad took dozens of photos when we were little of us Wunrow boys sitting on cannons and saluting. I immediately sent the photos to Aaron and Seth since this is a running joke that the three of us share.

Right at the end of the day we met an elderly couple out on a walk, who we stopped to talk with. They were so impressed and encouraging of what we've accomplished so far. That boosted our moods a bit. And then later, we met a lady walking her two rescue dogs, a big white one and a big black one. We stopped to talk with her about dogs for a while, and that little bit of normal conversation about something other than the trail, and the mud, and the miles, seemed to help a bit, too.

Leslie's Journal Entry:

. . . When you slip in the mud and brace yourself with your arm and land your face in a cozy patch of nettles! Yeah, that's me.

Tuesday, October 3, 2017, Hiking Day 43
Fishguard to Pwll Deri
(Stayed at Schoolhouse Hostel in Trefin)
9½ miles; Total – 496½ miles

Great day! Awesome weather. Mostly sunny.

Amazingly beautiful trail along high cliffs. The muddy trail was pretty dried out today. And we ended up walking with just day packs. And we saw adult and baby seals on five or six different secluded beaches. Very cool.

Before I forget. We just walked into the Ship Inn in Trefin, the only placed to eat in Trefin, as there are no stores and no other restaurants. It is a 200-plus-year-old pub. We're having two proper beers, local brews from Blue Stone Brewery in Pembrokshire. There is a very limited pub menu, as always. I ordered "Welsh faggots" with mushrooms. I asked the bartender lady what Welsh faggots were, and I didn't really understand what he said, but she said it was very good. So, we'll see. Leslie ordered a fish pie made with fresh local seafood. We're staying in Trefin tomorrow night, too, so we'll be here for dinner again. There are fresh local mussels and a few other things that look good on the menu to look forward to tomorrow.

The Schoolhouse Hostel, where we're staying tonight and to-morrow night, is pretty cool. The lady who runs it, Jill, was really friendly and funny. It's not a regular sanctioned hostel, but a private one with a nice communal kitchen, little living room with lots of books, and maybe six rooms. It looks like we are the only ones here tonight.

A basic breakfast comes with the room, porridge, toast, jam, and coffee. And we ordered a packed lunch as well for the next two days. All necessary since, again, there is no store here in Trefin, and the only other food option is the Ship Inn.

We got dropped off in Fish Guard by our "Carrot Taxi" driver's wife this morning. She'd just worked a night shift at a group home for developmentally disabled youth, and was giving us a ride on her way home go head to bed. She also picked us up this afternoon in Pwll Deri at 3:30pm, so I know she didn't get much sleep.

Again, it was a great walk today. Seeing all the seals hidden in the rocky beaches was cool. We walked three hours straight to a big white lighthouse at Stumble Head. It was about seven miles into our day. The sun was out and we laid on the grass and had our sandwiches and crisps and Ho Hos. It was nice to be able to just relax on the grass and in the sun. Most days it is rainy and cold, so our lunches are pretty quick affairs. A longer relaxing lunch stop is a rarity.

The last couple of miles to Pwll Deri were just stupendous! High, sheer cliffs and views all the way to St. David's Head, maybe 15 miles ahead. There is a youth hostel in Pwll Deri, advertised as the most beautiful scenic hostel in all of Wales. It's closed right now for some reason, but it sits up high above the cliffs. It would be an amazing place to stay someday. Or to come back to someday as a volunteer hostel host.

One thing about the Schoolhouse Hostel where we are staying: it is very eclectically decorated. Our room has a Marilyn Monroe theme. There are all kinds of antique children's toys, old movie posters, mannequin heads, and other eccentric things in every window sill and on every shelf. I love it. Not like the typical Ikea-furnished youth hostel. Our room is great. The price is relatively cheap. I'm glad we are here for two nights.

Leslie's Journal Entry:

We have been walking for six straight weeks now. Woot!

Jon says I am best at the "falling game." I am winning three to zero in that one.

He is winning the *Guess What Time It Is* game; the *How Much is Dinner Going to Cost* game; and, as previously mentioned, the *Guess What Color the Next Car is Going to Be* game.

I missed Gizmo today. I just want to lay around with her pawing on my belly while binge watching Season 4 of *Orange is the New Black*.

Wednesday, October 4, 2017, Hiking Day 44
Pwll Deri to Trefin
(Night #2 at Schoolhouse Hostel in Trefin)
10½ miles; Total – 507 miles

We're back at the Ship Inn pub in Trefin. It's the only place that serves dinner (there is also a café that serves breakfast and lunch in Trefin), so we don't have a choice. But dinner last night was fine enough. It is really windy and cold outside tonight. It's a few hundred-yard walk from the hostel to the pub and it is making me think that I may need to start wearing long pants one of these days! The highs this week have been around 55 degrees, but with winds over 20mph, it feels cold. It is October after all, so it probably won't be getting any warmer.

So much of our anticipation or dread about hiking the next day, so much of our enjoyment (or not) of the day while we are hiking is based on the weather. Rain, wind, sun, calm. It really dictates the level of enjoyment for the day. Yesterday was mostly sunny with a wind around 15mph. A very enjoyable day. Today, it was cloudy all day, but no rain, and windier. Like a consistent 20mph. Still a good day but not as enjoyable or as memorable. Tomorrow is supposed to be sunny and windy. So, we're looking forward to a good day of hiking without rain.

The day was full of seeing little seal pups on the beach again today. I just Googled it and seals give birth on the beach in the cold fall and winter months. The moms give birth on the beach, hang around for a month or so feeding the little white furry babies, and then the moms head back into the ocean and the pups lay on the beach alone for another two weeks, building up the courage and strength to head off into the ocean on their own.

We passed several isolated beaches that were down below the steep cliffs and our trail, some with a dozen or more huge fat seals, brown, black, or mottled. Some beaches have several moms with their little white babies next to them, and then we saw beaches that just had five or six little white blobs, laying there all my themselves. I was wondering why that was until I read about it.

We actually saw a few hikers on the trail today. We haven't seen many over the last several days. This section of the trail in Pembrokshire, yesterday and today, are pretty well known for the views and steep cliffs and seal colonies.

Simon: Yesterday we saw a guy ahead of us on the trail near the lighthouse who was carrying a big backpack, a rolled-up foam pad, and wearing jeans. We knew instantly that he didn't look organized enough to be a through-hiker. Today we caught up with him and he's doing a five-day hike, and camping along the way. Today his bulky sleeping bag was hanging halfway out of its stuff sack. Leslie mentioned after we met him that he looked like he was falling apart. He said he'd lost his hat so he was hearing a hand-knit stocking cap. Sort of an old guy. But I definitely give him credit for being out here and totally self-sufficient. Super nice.

Margaret: We met a solo hiker coming towards us. She seemed about our age, and was from Seattle. She's only the second person we've met in the past 44 days who is also from the U.S. She goes on a one- or two-week hiking trip every year, using a travel agency to plan her hike, book lodging, and transfer her bags every day. When she met us, she said, "Are you the two who are hiking 800 miles?" And then, "You're the two hikers from the U.S., right?" We weren't sure how she knew of us, but the momentary fame was a little flattering. She's on a one-week trip, has a good friend who lives in Bloomington, Indiana, and hates Trump as much as we do. So much in common.

Ali: We met Ali at breakfast at the hostel this morning. She's good friends with Sue, the owner, and is staying for a while to get out of the city of Bristol. She seemed really nice. She had her dog Myrtle with her in the hostel kitchen, who, while we talked, proceeded to pee on the kitchen floor. Dogs are treated like humans and babies in the U.K. including Wales. Welcome in restaurants and pubs (and kitchens) almost everywhere.

Leslie's Journal Entry:

I wasted 30 minutes of our walking time trying to get the perfect selfie with a horse.

500 miles today!

We met a hiker from the U.S. today who grew up in Indiana. Weird.

Met a British hiker. A guy with a weird name. Just kidding . . . his name was Simon.

Thursday, October 5, 2017, Hiking Day 45
Trefin to White Sands
(Lodging – Couch House in St. David's)
11 miles; Total – 518 miles

Sue, the hostel manager has made us great lunches yesterday and today. Great bread, and mine had salmon spread. Leslie has feta cheese and tomato, I think. Plus, we each got a "sausage roll," bag of crisps, juice box, fruit, and a couple of cookies. It was a lunch to look forward to. I liked mine so much yesterday that I asked for the exact same thing today.

We had a fairly sunny day for most of our 11-mile hike. It was windy all day. Blowing around 20mph consistently. But I'd rather have wind and sun, than wind and rain.

We saw lots and lots of newborn seal pups, laying on rocky beaches far below the trail in several places. In one spot, the trail dropped down to within 15 yards or so of three furry, white seal pups, and two big mommas. The nearest mom kept a close eye on us with her little jet-black eyes. The pups were oblivious to us, just lying there and occasionally fidgeting. Pretty cool to see them so close up. Our taxi driver at the end of the day today told us that once the babies are born, and old enough to flop down the beach and into the water, the seals aren't seen again on the beaches until birthing time next year. They stay in the water their entire lives except when they are having babies and being birthed.

Our trail guidebook used the words, "Neolithic" and "prehistoric" and "iron age" several times to describe walls, mounds, and circular depressions that we passed. I'm not exactly sure what the definition of any of those three time periods is, but I know they mean "old." Towards the end of the hike that circled around a piece of land that jutted out into the sea, called St. David's Head, I was watching intently for a "Neolithic burial chamber" that apparently is 5,500 years old. But I never saw it. We've passed a couple of others that were a ways off the trail, and we haven't bothered to wander over to find them. The landscape here is covered in dense shrubs and gorse, and is very rocky, so it's hard to pick out specific 5,500-year-old stone structures. But this one was supposed to be close to the trail. I need to look up "Neolithic" and "iron age" online to see what was going on back then.

Our hike ended at White Sands Beach, a beautiful fine-sand beach, like ones we were seeing a few weeks ago. We caught a taxi two and a half miles to the "smallest city in the U.K.," St. David's. Apparently, a "city" is designated as such if it has a cathedral. The cathedral here at St. David's has been around for a long time. We were told that a pope in the 1200s decreed that anyone who visited this cathedral twice in a single day would receive the same blessings as if he/she had visited the Vatican in Rome. Not sure what the blessings are? But I may pop over there twice tomorrow afternoon, after our 13-mile hike. I may need a blessing after that.

We bought two pasties from a guy in front of our B&B, and then some pickles, wine, beer, and caramel fudge at the little store nextdoor, and then settled into our little two-story cottage that is attached to the back of the Coach House B&B. It is a nice cozy space. My right hip is really aching tonight after sitting around for a couple of hours. Tomorrow we have 13 miles, but only with day packs.

Leslie's Journal Entry:

Seriously, some pretty stunning, jaw-dropping scenery, and so many cute, fat seal pups. I want one now.

Jon is sort of obsessed with seeing an ancient fort and burial chamber. He seems disappointed when we get to the spots where they are supposed to be, and it is just a grassy mound since they are around 5,000 years old and this is just what is left.

Friday, October 6, 2017, Hiking Day 46
White Sands to Solva
(Night #2 at the Couch House in St. David's)
13 miles; Total – 531 miles

Time is relative. Einstein's theory of general relativity describes a space-time continuum, and states something like, time slows the faster an object travels. Einstein said that time is a "relative" concept. Moving clocks run slower as their velocity increases, and at the speed of light (186,000 miles per second) time stops all together.

So, in terms of hiking the Wales Coast Path, time also seems very relative. Some days, time and miles fly by. It seems like we just started walking and I check the time and two and a half hours have gone by. Other days, time elongates. It drags. We walk, and walk, and walk, and time seems to have slowed down. The clock just doesn't seem to move at all.

I'm starting to realize that time is more of a psychological concept. I'm 21 years old, and turn around twice, and now I'm 56 years old. Where did the time go? And how is it that it passed so quickly? Time flies when you're having fun. After a long day's hike, we just want to sit around in our B&B or apartment and have the evening last forever, because tomorrow morning we have to get up and put on our packs and stinky shoes and socks and walk again. But invariably the time flies by and it is bedtime, and then time to hike again before we know it.

It seems like I can control time, or at least my perception of whether time is passing slowly or quickly with my mind. I can slow time way down when I focus on each passing moment and become aware of each minute in the hour. When I become present in the moment. And I can speed time up by letting my mind wander and day dream about future adventure . . . just let my mind drift, and before I know it, and hour or two and several miles have passed. So, time is relative to more than just the speed of an object, as Einstein proved. It is also relative to our frame of mind, relative to our mood, relative to our attitude.

Lately I've found myself thinking a lot about projects I want to get done and things I want to do when we get home. Roast some coffee; build a railing to replace the broken one next to our outdoor stairs; buy a hot tub; go visit Seth and Shauna; move the Stairmaster to my office; etc. etc. And I've been thinking a lot more about work and work-related things that I need to get done. With 46 days of hiking done and about 29 days to go, more or less, my thoughts are gravitating more and more to being home.

Today was the sunniest and calmest day we've had in a very long time. No wind at all. Sometimes it seemed so unusually quiet because we are so used to having the wind in our ears all day long. And although there were dozens of ups and downs, I only had my daypack on, and the 13 miles seemed to fly by. Thirteen miles is a long way. But the time passed quickly and so did the miles.

We stopped along the trail around mile nine for a nice lunch stop. When we got up to go again, a couple passed, and we started to talk. They are doing long day hikes in the area. The guy dropped that they'd hiked twenty miles yesterday. So, I couldn't resist and said we were hiking the whole Coastal Path. The guy said, "Oh wow, all 140 miles of the Pembrokshire Coast?" "No, we hit our 500-mile mark a few days ago." He immediately and literally bowed to us and said, "That is incredible. I am not worthy." Damn right you're not.

So, we found out, somehow, I think from a taxi driver, that the guy who owns the B&B in St. David's where we are staying again tonight, used to be the chef for the King of Jordan. That is pretty wild. So, I had high expectations for breakfast. And he delivered. We had awesome omelettes this morning for breakfast.

Our 13 miles ended in the cute little village of Solva this afternoon. Great day. Great weather. Great hike. Dinner blew. We bought microwaveable Indian food that was lousy, and the bottle of wine we opened seemed watery to me. But we finished off dinner with a pint of Häagen-Dazs cookie dough ice cream. So that saved the disastrous dinner.

Leslie's Journal Entry:

Our B&B host acts like we should be honored to be in his presence. Does he know who WE are?

Jon said we should eat out, and then said pizza sounded good, and then tried to talk me into a rotisserie chicken to eat in our room (we have no plates or cutlery). We settled on microwave Indian food because we only eat Indian every other freakin' day. But to be fair, we have not yet tried frozen Indian from the grocery. Never again.

Saturday, October 7, 2017, Hiking Day 47
Solva to Broad Haven
(Night #1 in Pembroke)
11 miles; Total – 542 miles

Okay, here we go on the much-pondered historic time references:

> Prehistoric – Use of first stone tools, 3.5 million years ago
> Neolithic (New stone age) – 15,200 BC - 2,500 BC

Bronze Age – 2,500 - 800 BC
Iron Age – 800 BC (2,800 years ago)

These time period references have been plaguing me as we walked past several forts that were built in the Iron Age, so 2,800 years ago. There was one fort we walked past yesterday that was a series of long, high grassy walls, probably originally made of stones, with a series of inner walls, and outer walls. I wonder what people living in this area were like 2,800 years ago. And those illusory Neolithic tombs that we've passed at least three of, but haven't seen a single one? These tombs are over 5,000 years old! Pretty wild.

Today was another good hiking day. We went 11 miles and there was a surprising lot of ups and downs. Lots of stair climbing up the sides of steep ravines, and lots of knee jarring downhill steps, too. But the wind was at our backs. It was cloudy with no rain. So, a perfect walking day with our ever-growing backpacks.

What made the day great was having a few things to look forward to along the route. At mile five and a half, we dropped into the village of Newgale where there was a beautiful 3km long sandy beach and a cute little coffee shop where we stopped in and got yummy lattes. Then in two more miles we took a brief rest break in Nolton Haven, where there was another nice beach. I was ready for a lunch break there. But Leslie wanted nothing to do with our same old snack and lunch food of bread and peanut butter, beef jerky, processed cheese, Ho Hos, and chips. I got crabby because Leslie wanted to push on another mile and a half to a hotel where we thought there might be a restaurant. I was like, "Yea, we'll get there at 2pm and they'll be done serving lunch." I also tried, "They're probably just serving cream tea and won't even have lunch." Leslie did an awesome job of completely ignoring my crabbiness and just kept on walking.

We eventually got to the Druidstone Hotel, perched high up on a cliff, and it was amazing!! A cool, funky feel, great artwork, amazing views, and the homemade food was awesome. I got some barbecued wings, and a lamb and chickpea vegetable soup. Leslie got a great quiche and salad. We both got incredible homemade coleslaw and fresh baked bread. I even had a pint of a locally brewed IPA. The bottom line? Leslie was right to push us and not give in to my whining.

We are back to sandy beaches again. Our trail passed at least four nice, fine-grained beaches with no rocks. Not too many people out on a Saturday since its October 7th and pretty cloudy and breezy. But there were a few hearty souls swimming, walking their dogs, and a couple of parasailers and kite boarders.

When we got to Broad Haven, we grabbed an expensive (£40!!) taxi to Pembroke. The trail for these next few days sort of circles around the Pembroke and we loved the idea of unpacking and spreading out in one location for a while. So, this was a perfect spot where we could have a single home base for several days. But the taxis will be expensive to get back and forth to the trail. The place where we are staying has a full kitchen and we'll save something by making our own dinners and breakfasts the next few days.

Leslie's Journal Entry:

Jon didn't want to go to a restaurant for lunch today because he was suffering from some man-o-pause brought on by hunger (which I can relate to, so I did not smack him like I wanted to). He wanted to eat what we had. I said, "That's fine. Moldy bread dipped in peanut butter, with pepperoni sticks, and Ho Hos sounds good to me, too." He just kept walking.

Best lunch ever! You're welcome.

Sunday, October 8, 2017, Hiking Day 48
Broad Haven to Morfoes Sands
(Night #2 in Pembroke)
12½ miles; Total – 554½ miles

Another beautiful day, with relatively easy hiking. No road walking, but the cliffs are not as high, so the ups and downs are shorter. The sun was out for most of the day, and the trail wasn't muddy at all! For the first couple of miles, the tall grasses that we passed through were wet from dew, so our socks and shoes were soaked early on. But that's just being nit-picky.

The trail is starting to wear on both of us. The end is still too far off to be excited about. We have probably 27 more hiking days? I think that when we get under three weeks to go, and then two weeks, the end will be in sight.

First thing this morning, a lady in Middle Haven stopped us and asked, "Are you hiking the entire trail?" Totally out of the blue. We told her she was a good guesser, and she told us that a few months ago, her daughter hiked the entire 180-mile Pembrokshire Coast Path. That's what she meant by "the entire trail." When we told her that we'd actually started in Chester 48 days ago, she was stunned. I think it's hard for people to comprehend hiking for 48 straight days, or for 550 miles, when they are out for a four- or five-mile day hike, or at most, stringing five-day hikes together into a 50 or 60 mile adventure.

Today we again walked by three or four amazingly beautiful sandy beaches. Jagged, steep, rocky cliffs for a few miles, and then all of the sudden, to me anyway, we'd came upon a perfect, fine-sand beach with a footpath or a series of stairs leading down to it.

Sometimes these beautiful beaches have a car park close by, and sometimes there is a trail leading to a beach that requires a 15- to 30-minute walk. We've noticed a couple of times today, that we'd be hiking for an hour or more and not see a soul through sections of trail that are overgrown and unused. And after a while we'll start to see a couple of day hikers as the trail improves, and then a few more walkers with their dogs, and we know that we're getting close to a car park or an access trail to a beach. I don't think too many people venture very far from their cars.

Today is Sunday and a sunny Sunday, so there were a few people out and about. We even saw four adults, around our age, in their swimming suits out playing in the waves. Even though it is sunny, the temp only got up to sixty or so, and the water is way colder than that.

At one point we saw a castle off in the distance. We later read that it was built in the mid-1800s and now is an exclusive condo community with an indoor pool, restaurant, cottages, and condos in the castle.

Back to our Airbnb at 39 Main Street in Pembroke. The taxi from Morloes Sands back to our place was £52!! That's around $65US!! So, we'll have to pay that again tomorrow morning to get back out to where we left off. But we are loving being able to stay in the same place for three nights in a row; make our own meals (tonight we had grilled cheese and tomato basil soup); and have room to spread out, dry out, and not have to pack up in the morning. So, it's worth the extra taxi cost.

Leslie's Journal Entry:

Please refer to Jon's well-thought-out journal entry for today while I have a drink.

Monday, October 9, 2017, Hiking Day 49
Morloes Sands to Sandy Haven to Milford Haven
13 miles; Total – 567½ miles

Leslie is still struggling a bit with motivation and just enjoying the days. She's sick of hiking and spends a lot of time thinking about Goldie, Gizmo, and Gabby, and just being back home. She has no interest in quitting and is committed to the goal of finishing, but the walking gets old, and despite the beauty, is kind of boring after a while. It doesn't bother me as much . . . that need to be back home that is. I'm not sure why. I think it's because I'd rather be doing this every day, getting great exercise, than sitting at my desk in my office at home. After doing something for 49 straight days, it is just a challenge to stay motivated and keep going.

Leslie has developed a bit of a toothache, too. It started a few days ago. Not constant, but painful. I think we've narrowed it down to a cracked tooth or maybe loose crown. Today, after our 13 miles, we stopped in a pharmacy and got some tooth repair stuff, just to cover the crack, but it didn't stick. Tomorrow we may just walk into a dentist and see if they have a product that can be "painted" on the cracked area to see if it helps.

The biggest news on our hike today is that I woke up to a Packers win over the Cowboys! When I went to bed last night, the Packers were losing 21 to six before the end of the first half. Three Cowboy possessions resulting in three touchdowns. Three Packer possessions resulting in a touchdown with a missed extra point. At about 4am, I woke up and checked my phone and saw the headline, "65-Yard Drive in the Final 1:13 Give Packers the Win." So, I spent this morning watching highlights of the game for an hour. Amazing! Aaron Rodgers was nothing short of amazing. Down by three points with 1:13 to go in the game. And they win with a touchdown with 10 seconds left on the clock. Seth and I texted about it a bit today. He watched it, and said it was a nailbiter, and that I would have hated the game. Leslie says it is better for our marriage if I just watch the highlights of Packer games rather than watch the game live. She said I seem to get over the loses much more quickly that way, and she doesn't have to be around me being crabby during the three-hour game.

Oh, yeah, hiking today . . . almost forgot. . . . Pretty boring to be honest. The guidebook gave us an alternative early on to cut out about four and a half miles of our planned 14-mile day, so we took it, and then walked an extra three and a half miles at the end of the day, to make tomorrow's 17-miler, easier. So, now we "only" have 13½ miles to walk tomorrow.

The second half of the hike we entered Milford Haven Bay and walked past several large, docked ocean freighters, transporting liquified natural gas. Then we walked the first couple of miles into the city of Milford Haven. It is really only the second larger city that we've walked through. Tomorrow we'll be doing city walking pretty much the entire 14 miles, as we walk through the rest of Milford Haven, and then Llanstadwell and into Neyland, and finally Pembroke.

We also walk around a huge oil refinery tomorrow. I actually won't mind the city walking. It's a change of pace and there will be plenty to look at. And I promised Leslie we'd stop along the way for ice cream and lunch!! So, we have something to look forward to.

Leslie's Journal Entry:

Blisters, shin splints, knee pain, and now . . . toothache. Can you walk those out?

I am not going to survive this.

I'm falling apart.

Good news—I am in the lead on the *Guess What Time it Is* game!

Tuesday, October 10, 2017, Hiking Day 50
Milford Haven to Pembroke Castle
11 miles; Total – 578½ miles

HIKING DAY 50!!

That is a milestone!

Today's hike was half through wet grass and little-used trails going around power plants and natural gas lines, and the other half was walking on sidewalks through towns and cities.

"I just want to cuddle and watch *Project Runway*." This was Leslie's quote of the day. It's no secret that she's been struggling this last week with just wanting to be done and go home. Her code phrase for "I don't want to hike today" and "I just want to be done with our hike today" is "I just want to cuddle." Which, unfortunately, doesn't mean what it sounds like. It's become sort of a joke. Today she added the *Project Runway* part. Over the last few nights, we've been watching Season 15 episodes that have already aired. Two episodes each night on her iPad. So, the whole phrase really means, "Let's quit walking and get back to where we are staying so we can watch more episodes."

The highlight for the day? We went a few blocks off the route to McDonalds for lunch!! A Big Mac, large fries, and Diet Coke never tasted so good.

Leslie's Journal Entry:

I woke up this morning to find Jon sipping coffee in his chair in our little Pembroke apartment with his shirt on inside-out.

The sun came out while walking today and Jon took off his jacket. Hiking shirt still inside-out. Clearly, I am NOT the only one falling apart.

We went to McDonald's. It tasted like heaven and unicorns and puppies and all things wonderful.

Wednesday, October 11, 2017, Hiking Day 51
Pembroke Castle to Angle Beach
10 miles; Total – 588½ miles

We watch the weather very carefully every evening, every morning, and throughout the day. And the forecast for today was windy, steady 20 to 30mph winds with gusts to 50mph. And 100 percent chance of rain from 9am to 4pm. So, we were mentally prepared for the worst, and prepared to be soaked and cold all day long. The advantage of preparing for the worst is that sometimes it doesn't turn out that bad.

We walked out the front door of our Airbnb apartment around 9am and walked past the huge, intact Pembroke Castle. It was already blowing with gray clouds overhead. After the trail left the outskirts of Pembroke and another small village, it dropped to the seashore where the wind was really ripping and there was a light rain coming down.

The weather was so nasty that I decided we should take a more inland route on small one-lane rural roads that was about the same distance, but the high roadside hedges blocked the wind for several miles. There have been a few times that we've gone off the official trail route as noted in the guidebook that we've been following. Sometimes the guidebook gives an "official alternate" due to high tides, or diverting around an active military firing range (which we'll do tomorrow), and a few times I've picked an alternative route (like today), because of the weather or just because we need some kind of mental break.

I've struggled a little bit with whether this is "cheating" or not. But the bottom line is that we are still walking every step and not getting rides to skip anything. We are still slightly above where we should be at this point on the trail in terms of overall mileage, and are on track to walk a total of 880 miles (instead of the official trail mileage of 870) by the time we're done. And, it's our trip, no one else's, so we need to do what makes us happy. And the bottom line is, no one gives a shit what we do or what route we take.

So, we avoided a lot of the direct headwinds for most of the day, and it didn't really start to rain until around 11am. It was pretty nasty for a while with horizontal, driving rain, but not nearly as bad as it could have been. We eventually walked into the cute little village of Angle. A small harbor, an old stone church, and some small houses. No cafés or places to get out of the wind, so we sat on a stone bench in the covered entry of the church and ate our lunch. From there it was only a mile or so to the West Angle Beach, best known for the fact that a previously unknown starfish species was discovered there only twenty years ago.

We taxied back to our Airbnb apartment for our fifth night there! We are very settled into the place and have a routine there, so it'll be hard to leave in the morning. Part of my nightly routine throughout the entire trip is that I get out my laptop and do three or four hours of work before and after dinner (and now in between *Project Runway* episodes). I have lots and lots of work-related tasks, projects, grants, reports, etc., going on right now, and it is a little bit stressful to be juggling so many projects from Wales, and trying to keep it all going in a much-shortened work day.

Something that just came up is that I need to be in Washington, D.C., for a meeting from November 7th-9th, which means flying there on the 6th. Our current plan, if the last 24 days of our hike go perfectly, is to be done on November 4th and fly home (if there are seats available) on November 5th. Then leave for D.C. on the 6th, and then straight to Alaska from D.C. on the 10th. So, I started looking ahead in our guidebooks about how they lay out these final three and a half weeks to see if there is a way to pick up an extra day, just in case we can't get a flight out on November 6th. I need to book my D.C. flights now, as well as my flights to Alaska.

There is one four-day stretch of the trail that total only 41 miles. So, if we could hike those 41 miles in three days instead of four, that would help. And then there is another four-day stretch in the final section of the trail that is only 40½ miles. So, something there as well. It would mean lots of 13- and 14-mile days, instead of nines, 10s, and 11s, but if we could be finished an extra day or two early, that would help a lot. Leslie is all for giving it a try.

For now, we need to focus on our 12 to 13 miles tomorrow with our full packs. The first five miles are supposed to have a lot of ups and downs. I think the guidebook calls the section "challenging." Leslie just said, "It is not like we haven't done days like this before. We know how to put our heads down and just crank it out, and look up every once in a while to remember that we are in beautiful Wales."

Leslie's Journal Entry:

Jon says I have developed a bit of an attitude this last week or so. In an effort to be more positive, I am going to write all the most amazing things about hiking around a power plant in the rain and wind:

....

Thursday, October12, 2017, Hiking Day 52
Angle Beach to Bosherston (St. Govan's Country Inn)
13 miles; Total – 601½ miles

Today was sort of an odd day. The first four and a half miles or so, out of Angle Beach were up above sea cliffs and included a few very steep drops into little creek drainages, and then back up again. Thankfully, the trail was dry. If it was raining or muddy it would have been really slick. We got to walk along Freshwater West Beach for a half-mile or so, too. Just before we got to the beach, we again came upon our Seattle hiking friend, Margaret. She has a couple more days of her solo hike of the Pembrokshire Trail. She once again mentioned something cryptic about doing this trip to clear her head and allow her to move on from something. I'm guessing a divorce? Leslie thinks it's something else.

Leslie, for some dumb reason, only had a small pastie for breakfast, so she's been starving since the moment we started walking and after a couple of miles, slowed way, way down. I was actually getting kind of annoyed at how slow she was going. We'd been planning on hiking four and a half miles to this beach and then taking a snack break, but decided to stop sooner so Leslie could eat some sugar and protein and get her mojo back. Which worked.

While we stopped, a group of four older men walked up from behind us, all carrying backpacks about the size of two of ours. They are from somewhere near Bristol, England. They'd hiked the first six or seven days of the Pembrokshire Trail in April and have returned to hike the second half now in October. Really nice guys. The four of them also finished the Southwest Coast Path in sections over a four-year period.

The most interesting part of the day was that the last eight or nine miles bypassed a large military base that was doing live firing all day yesterday and today. So, we walked to the sounds of mortar fire and machine gun *rat-a-tat-tat* all day long. It was sort of weird actually. And it was all taking place just a kilometer or so away.

We walked alongside miles of barbed-wire fencing, and could hear military vehicles and tanks driving around. I even posed for a photo in front of a big tank that was parked by a gate into the base. When active firing exercises aren't taking place, the trail goes right through the middle of the military base. But today we had to detour way inland to walk round it all. Red cloth flags were flying at various entry points to warn hikers to stay out. It was a pretty long hiking day, so our feet and joints were sore. It was a 600mg Advil day for me.

We stayed at St. Govan's Country Inn in Bosherston. It is the only thing in this town other than a café. There is a pub and restaurant downstairs that was full of super young-looking G.I. Joe guys from the base. But by suppertime, it was just us, the four male hikers, and Margaret down for dinner and beers. Really the first time we've been around other long-distance trail hikers for an evening. We sat in the restaurant for a while before and after dinner, catching up on emails and doing work. Good day!!

Leslie's Journal Entry:

You should not set out to hike 13 miles on one little tasty cinnamon pinwheel for several reasons:

1. It takes exactly 12 steps into the hike before you are starving.

2. It takes 13 steps before you lose all energy and your cute husband says, "Come on, now. . . . We have a long way to go."

3. It takes 15 steps for that same husband to roll his eyes and say, "I knew it! I knew you should have eaten more. Why didn't you eat more? What all did you have? What? That is all you had?

Friday, October 13, 2017, Hiking Day 53
Bosherston to Manorbier
10½ miles; Total – 612 miles

We hit the 600-mile mark!!

Six hundred miles seems like such an amazing milestone. But that means we still have almost 270 miles to go!! We hit the 600-mile mark pretty much at the end of the hike today so we captured the moment by taking a photo of us laying in bed "sleeping" with Monkey Face holding a piece of paper that said, "We just hiked 600 miles!"

Today was windy all day long. A strong, damp wind blew, thankfully mostly from behind us. But it was constant all day long. There was a 50 percent chance of rain all day long as well, but thankfully we were on the dry side of that 50 percent today. We could see a lot of rain falling off in the distance around us, but we really only walked in the rain for a half-hour or so. Otherwise, just wind.

Breakfast at the St. Govan's Country Inn was our first Full English in a week. I've kind of missed the egg, bacon, sausage, toast, beans, fried tomato, and blood pudding. And we both noticed the difference on the trail this morning, too. A breakfast of granola and yogurt will last an hour before we are both starving. But a big breakfast like this morning lasted a good three hours, and even then we weren't super hungry.

The first few miles of the trail were right on the open coast and led around a point (Stackpole Head) with sheer rock fades that are internationally known to rock climbers. I heard someone in the pub last night say that there are 13 different rockclimbing guidebooks to the area. But it was super windy out there, so I didn't get too close to the edge, and we didn't linger.

Around mile four and a half, we passed a National Trust café like one we saw a month or so ago. Even though we only walked a few miles, we stopped in for some real coffee and a cocoa. It is so rare that we get to stop right along the trail to take an indoor, relaxing coffee break, so we just couldn't pass it up. The café was at the parking lot for access to Barafundle Bay and beach, "the winner of several Best Beach in Wales accolades." It was pretty, but I think we've seen lots of beautiful beaches on this trip.

More wind past a nude beach with no naked ninnies brave enough to be laying out in the high winds today. We stopped for lunch around 1:30pm and hunkered down behind a line of shrubs to get out of the wind. It was a wet, muddy, and pathetic spot to be sitting on the ground eating lunch, but at least we were out of the wind for a few minutes.

There is a little beach in Manorbier, the village where we're staying at the Castle Mead Hotel tonight. As we approached it, we saw 15 to 20 little black seal heads popping out of the water that we later realized were surfers in wet suits out catching the waves in this nasty blowing weather.

The Castle Mead is cute and cozy. There is a den with a fireplace that had a nice fire going. After we unpacked, and showered, and put on the same after-hiking clothes that we've been wearing now for two months, and caught up on emails and work, we went down to the den and sat by the fire.

Our new friend Margaret was up having her breakfast when we came down this morning. We all left Manorbier about the same time today, though Margaret showed up a couple of hours after we did. She stopped at the Castle Mead on the way to her B&B and asked if we'd join her for dinner tonight at our hotel. So, Leslie and I sat by the fire having a cozy drink while we waited for Margaret to arrive for dinner. And then we all sat for a while before we sent down for a nice evening and decent dinner. Margaret's last day of hiking is tomorrow and then she heads home to Seattle and her small publishing company.

Manorbier (or as Leslie says, "Man or beer? I'll choose beer") is known for its huge Manorbier Castle, built in the early 1100s!! A guy who ended up being known as Gerald of Wales was born here. Gerald was described as an "acclaimed clergyman, traveler, and prolific writer who penned 12 books that have survived to today. He was known for writing about the detailed observations of people, place and things during his travels through Wales. The description reminded me of my dad, "Gerald of Minnesota."

I just realized that I made an addition error and we've gone 11 miles further than I thought!!!!!! So, we actually hit the 600-mile mark at the end of yesterday. That's funny. Easiest 11 miles we've ever hiked.

Leslie's Journal Entry:

Today Jon said, "Maybe we can take a nap, and then watch *Project Runway* on our laptop." OMG! Is he perfect or what?

I will disregard his annoyance with me yesterday.

SECTION SIX:
CARMARTHEN BAY
& GOWER

Tenby to Swansea

Saturday, October 14, 2017, Hiking Day 54
Manorbier to Tenby (8 mi); Tenby to Saundersfoot (4½ mi)
12½ miles; Total – 624½ miles

Two cute tourist towns today: Tenby and Saunderfoot. Still a lot of tourists milling around, even though it's now mid-October. It is a Saturday, so that's part of it I'm sure.

The three most newsworthy events of today are:

(1) I realized this morning that I'd made an 11-mile addition error, and we actually hit the 600-mile mark two days ago, not yesterday. All that crazy celebrating and photos, and it was a day late. No wonder we were so tired today. We've gone 624 miles instead of 613!!

(2) I lost my wallet!! Including two credit cards, my driver's license, and $250 in cash. We walked eight miles to Tenby this morning and had been anticipating stopping into a Mountain Wearhouse store there for the past two weeks so Leslie could buy a lightweight down jacket. We've been talking about it for the past few days. Well, we walked into the large town, got to the Mountain Wearhouse store, put our packs down, and I started digging for my wallet in

the top flap of my backpack and realized that not only was it not in there, but I didn't remember seeing it this morning, or putting it anywhere.

We unpacked everything on the busy sidewalk in front of passing tourists. I called the little coffee house where we'd stopped yesterday morning by Barafundle Bay, and I called Castle Mead B&B where we'd just stayed.

And nothing! Rethinking every step.

Leslie has a couple credit cards so we were fine. But just a hassle thinking about canceling things and getting a new driver's license and just kicking myself for being so careless.

And then Leslie reminded me that I'd worn a coat to dinner last night. Bingo!! I dug out my fleece coat from the bottom of my pack, and there it was!! Phew.

(3) Mud, mud, mud. The last four and a half miles from Tenby to Saundersfoot was hilly, steep in some parts, and really muddy. Super slick, slow walking, and a challenge to stay in balance and not slip and fall. By the end of the day, my leg joints and lower back were killing me from slipping and sliding around. We both agreed that walking in this kind of mud in the hills is the worst type of trail to hike on.

Leslie's Journal Entry:

We had an unexpected sucky second half to our hike today, with a ton of steep climbs and muddy descents. As we rolled into town ... heading uphill, Jon said, "Okay, all I am going to say is that we are very close to our hotel." And when the hotel came into view, he said, "See the hotel that is dark with zero cars in the lot with no people in sight and that sign that says 'Vacancies'? Yup, that's it."

I thought that was funny.

I just washed my hair with hand lotion. WTF?

Sunday, October 15, 2017, Hiking Day 55
Saundersfoot to Pendine Sands
9 miles; Total – 633½ miles

A breeze of a walk. And fun, actually. The first mile or so out of Saundersfoot, from right out the front door of our hotel, was on roads and walkways along the ocean. Flat. Nice. We walked with day packs since we'll be back at our Saundersfoot hotel again tonight. The walkway to Wiseman's Bridge, another touristy coastal village, had a dozen or more joggers and dog walkers on it this morning.

At Wiseman's Bridge, we headed down to the beach and walked until we hit some big rocks uncovered at low tide. The guidebook didn't suggest an alternate low tide route along the beach, but we decided to try it. The high tide was in about three hours, so we headed out across the sand, and then over several hundred yards of rocky and slippery tide pools. I was a little worried that Leslie wouldn't handle the slippery rocks well, but she had fun climbing over the rocks and skirting the little tide pools. We eventually hit a huge sandy beach in front of the village of Amroth.

I'd been seeing the name "Amroth Castle" for two weeks because it's the end point of the 187-mile Pembrokshire Coastal Path. Probably the most popular and traveled part of the entire Wales Coast Path, and a noteworthy accomplishment for the people we met, like Margaret, who hiked this section over 15 days, or the "boys" as we refer to them, who hike just half of this section over the past week.

We eventually reached a sign that said something like, "Congrat-

ulations. You've completed the 300km Pembrokshire Coast Path."
And another sign across the street that said, "Amroth Castle." But
there was no castle in sight. Just an old stone wall, behind which
was a huge caravan park. I sort of got a chuckle out of this much
anticipated "castle" ending up being a trailer park.

After a mile or two of trail walking, we got to another more remote beach. Again, the trail guidebook didn't mention the beach
as a low tide option. I think it's because it was a little tricky getting
down to it, and it was possible to get stuck down there when the
tide comes back. We decided to give it a try and it was amazing.
The beach stretched for about two miles beneath towering black
cliffs with a dozen or so sea caves carved into the black stone walls.
No one was there because there's no road access to the beach. Really cool. We passed two old stone houses sitting further up the
shore. Really remote and isolated. We eventually hiked up off the
beach through a bunch of loose rounded stones to an old trail that
led back to our official path. We supposedly passed some "Neolithic burial chambers amid overgrown gorse bushes." But I never saw
them. I'm still hoping to see at least one Neolithic burial chamber
before this hike is over!

Our hike ended in a little touristy village full of caravan trailers
called Pendine Sands. And from there we took an expensive taxi
ride back to Saundersfoot. Nine miles without big packs still took
about five hours to cover.

For dinner, we went to a place called the Beachside Barbecue and I
had a great IPA, brewed and bottled in Tenby.

Leslie's Journal Entry:

Monday, October 16, 2017, Hiking Day 56
Pendine Sands to St. Clears (Night #1 in Carmrthen)
11½ miles; Total – 645 miles

Today was one windy fucking day! Or one fucking windy day. Either way.

The weather reports last night were predicting gale force winds along the coast as a rare tropical storm slammed all of Ireland today (over 100mph winds in Ireland this afternoon we learned, and already three people reported killed). My little smart phone weather app showed steady winds of 45 to 50mph pretty much all day today.

The good news was that the trail went way inland from Saunders-foot, along an estuary. So, we were fairly protected from the wind for most of the day. If we'd been on the coast today and high up on the cliffs like we often are, it would've been dangerous.

As it was, we got hammered by blasts of strong wind as we crossed open fields throughout the day, and this was after we'd traveled several miles inland. The sound of the high winds followed all day long, as it whistled through overhead trees.

The 11 miles was fairly level. A few ups and downs, but nothing bad. No matter how long we go with our big packs on, my feet and joints always end up hurting after a while.

The most interesting thing we saw today was the Laugharne Castle in the little village of Laugharne. The castle dates back to the 12th century and is falling down, but still with large parts intact. Apparently, the famous poet Dylan Thomas spent his last few years here. So, there were signs all over the place pointing to "Dylan Thomas' Boathouse," "Dylan Thomas' Writing Shed," and "Dylan Thomas Birthday Walk Trail." Seriously. His birthday walk trail!

Little bits of his poetry are printed on benches and signs all over the place. It was sort of odd and funny at the same time. His boathouse seemed to get the most signage and attention for some reason. I was looking for a sign to point to "Dylan Thomas' Shithouse," but never saw one.

Another big day done. We're getting there. Nineteen days to go if we don't try to consolidate any future days. We're both pretty motivated to try to consolidate some days to pick up one or two days over the next 19. We'll see.

Leslie's Journal Entry:

I'm ready for a new sport. Like sliding on innertubes or jumping up and down in the waves . . . in the Caribbean.

Tuesday, October 17, 2017, Hiking Day 57
St. Clears to 3½ miles past Llansteffan
(Night #2 in Carmarthen)
13½ miles; Total – 658½ miles

Amazing! I'm speechless. A stunning win.

Towards the end of today we did our last three miles walking along a road. So, Leslie suggested we play the *What Color Car is Coming Next?* game to make the time go by more quickly. Leslie vaulted to a quick three to one lead. We'd talked several days ago about adding a new rule that if you pick an obscure car color, like pink or yellow or orange, you'd get extra points if you guessed correctly. We agreed that if someone picked one of these colors, they'd get an immediate five points!

So, Leslie, feeling cocky with her lead, picked orange and sure as shit, the next vehicle to come towards us was an orange truck!! We both about shit ourselves!! In the blink of an eye she was ahead eight to one. I scraped and clawed my way to a nine to six deficit, but she won on a black car. It was an amazing win, and before we knew it, we'd walked the final three miles. Works every time. It must be hilarious to see us walking down a rural road screaming out colors and high-fiving and doing little victory dances with our backpacks on along the side of the road.

I'm sitting in bed at the moment (8:53pm) and both of my legs still burn from walking through several patches of stinging nettles earlier today. Showering seems to have made them sting even more!

I forgot to mention that yesterday when we were leaving Saundersfoot to catch the bus to Pendine to start our hike, we stopped and got coffees at a little coffee shop around the corner from the bus stop. Leslie got talking with the lady in the shop about our trip and as we left, she gave Leslie a package of fresh Welsh cakes as a gift. So nice. We really appreciated that. Little gifts like that mean a lot.

We've decided to try to squeeze the next four days of hiking—according to the trail guidebook—into three days so we can pick up one day and hopefully get home one day sooner. The guidebook section for today was 10 miles, St. Clears to Llansteffan. So, we hiked those 10 miles, stopped for lunch at a little snack stand by the beach and below the Llansteffan Castle, and then hiked another three abd a half miles. Tomorrow, the guidebook recommends a nine-mile day, of which we just walked the first three and a half, and my plan is for us to go a total of 14!! And then we do more than 15 the next day, which will get us one day ahead.

So far, so good.

The last few days, my ass-crack has really been chaffing. Like at the beginning of the hike, when I put Vaseline in my crack every day for a while. I then switched to putting baby powder between the old cheeks. But neither of us have put either product in our asses for a month or more. But the last few days . . . I'm not sure what's going on down there. Lately, around mile nine or 10 I've been feeling some chaffing, which, if left unaddressed quickly turns into raw skin that hurts like hell and takes days to heal. Not fun and painful. Take it from an expert.

Anyway, I forgot to put some Johnson's in my crack when we stopped for lunch, and shortly after starting back up, I knew that I needed some relief. The problem was, we were walking along a road with no easy turn-offs.

So, while on the move, along the road, I dumped a bunch of powder in my hand and then quickly shoved my hand in my pants and slapped the powder between my cheeks. Bullseye.

Leslie couldn't believe I'd done it in broad daylight. So, just for good measure, and to gross her out even more, I dumped a bunch more Johnson's in my hand, waited for a couple of cars to go by, and gave my crack another powdering!! The problem was that we'd left the hand sanitizer in our room. Oops.

Leslie's Journal Entry:

Today was a pretty fall-like day. It makes me want pumpkin bread, pumpkin muffins, pumpkin scones, and pumpkin lattes while carving pumpkins and roasting pumpkin seeds.

Wednesday, October 18, 2017, Hiking Day 58
3½ miles past Llansteffan to Carmaethen – 5½ miles
Carmaethen to Ferryside – 8½ miles
14 miles; Total – 672½ miles

Today was one of those days where, halfway through, we were both saying things like, "I can't wait to stand in a hot shower when we get done," and "I can't wait to peel these wet shoes and socks off," and "I can't wait to put on clean, dry clothes," and "I can't wait to crawl under the cozy comforter on our hotel bed." That tells you all you need to know about today.

We also started the day by planning to find a decent restaurant somewhere in Carmaethen, and maybe even walking around the downtown shopping area a little bit after our hike today. But we ended up with "We may not ever leave our room once we are done hiking." That gives you an idea of how our thinking changed over today's 14-mile hike and seven solid hours of walking.

Hiking 14 miles is a long damn way! I don't care who you are, and how old or young, or how heavy or light your pack is. It's a long damn way.

After going five and a half miles into Carmaethen, we stopped at the train station and got muffins and something to drink. A light drizzle had just started and it was a cold morning. We could see our breath for this first time on this trip. About two miles after that 20-minute break, we stopped for five minutes in some little kid's school bus shelter and coated our ass-cracks with a double dose of baby powder, and then around mile 11 we stopped for another 20-minutes to eat our lame lunch while balancing our butts on the edge of the concrete base of a kissing gate. And those were about the only breaks we took for the entire 14 miles.

I took a sum total of one photo today. One. A closeup of our mud-caked shoes after we'd both just gone ankle deep in a slimy combo of red mud and cow shit.

On a different note. . . . How hard is it to put salad dressing on a damn salad??? Of all of the salads we've had during our two months of walking through Wales, and the two months we spent on the Southwest Coast Path in England, maybe only 10 percent of the salads come with any kind of dressing, and that's only a light glaze of vinegar and oil. Maybe. Countless times, I've asked nicely at restaurants, "Does the salad come with dressing?" And the majority of the time the answer is "no." The rare "yes" results in a few drops of vinegar or God knows what sprinkled on top.

The other day we were somewhere—I can't remember where—and I asked about dressing, and the answer was that the large salad, like ordering a salad as a main course, came with dressing. But the small dinner salad didn't. "So, can I please get dressing on my side salad," I asked again? "No. I'm sorry." WTF?

Two more things about today's long 14-mile hike:

1) We got to ride the train back from Ferryside to Carmaethen at the end of our hike. That was fun.

2) I actually thought of three things. It drizzled a light, misty drizzle for most of the afternoon, and there was only a 15 to 20 percent chance of rain in the forecast.

3) Shit, what was the third thing . . . ? We had our nasty laundry done by the hotel today? No. . . . We ended up not leaving the hotel to walk around town, and had a relatively nasty dinner at the hotel? No. . . . We saw a little kid at the train station this morning that was so excited when he saw the train coming that the almost peed his pants? No. . . . I can't think of what the third thing was.

Leslie's Journal Entry:

Today I got my head stuck in a sticker bush. I pulled and pulled, trying to get my head free, while Jon, up ahead of me, laughed.

Once I broke free, I said, "Thanks a lot for your help!"

He said, "Well, I wasn't going to backtrack!"

What we do to not have to walk one extra step.

Thursday, October 19, 2017, Hiking Day 59
Ferryside Railroad Station to Kidwelly – 5½ miles
Kidwelly to 3-miles before Burry Port – 7½ miles
13 miles; Total – 685½ miles

Sort of a boring hike today. Mostly road walking from Ferryside to Kidwelly and then some road and paved walkways from Kidwelly through a Forest Park to an amazing and immense sandy beach. And finally, some beach walking for the final three miles.

Road walking really takes its toll on our feet and joints. After a few miles of walking on pavement with packs on our backs, our feet start to ache, and then after a few more miles, it is my knee and hip joints that start to throb. Walking on grass, sand, dirt, or even gravel is much less painful and requires far fewer daily Advil. I'd planned to stop in Kidwelly to buy food for lunch, but we walked right through the middle of it and never saw a store. So, we ate some of our lame snacks around 11:15am on the outskirts of Kid-welly while Leslie bandaged up her two blistering little toes. It's so weird to be developing blisters 685 miles into the trip, and for no apparent reason. I took the opportunity to put a double layer of baby powder between my cheeks. Again, odd that I'm having this chaffing problem after two months of hiking.

We stopped around 1pm for "lunch" which was just Round Two of the snacks we've been carrying around for a week now: a bag of pulverized vinegar and salt chips, beef jerky, dry roasted peanuts, a yummy vanilla frosted oat bar, and a small cheese wheel. That was about it.

During the beach section, it started to rain. It was actually sup-posed to rain for most of the day, so we lucked out. But the last 75 minutes or so, the wind blew rain into our faces and we both got pretty soaked. We did see some interesting critters on the beach including another small Portuguese Man-of-War; some shells we haven't seen before; lots of big jelly fish blobs; a good sized dead crab; and even something that looked like the washed-up carcass of a dead sheep.

Otherwise, it was heads-down walking to keep the rain and wind out of our faces. I actually wore my wool hat and gloves most of the day and for the first time. So, it's definitely getting colder these later days of October.

Right now, we are settled in a mini apartment in Burry Port. It's really nice. Newly remodeled. Burry Port is a cute little seaside village. We went to the co-op and bought food for lunch tomorrow and some wine for tonight. We also stopped in a bakery for breakfast treats, buns for sandwiches, and dessert for tonight. I got a pizza from a place across the street from where we are staying, and we had pizza and wine for dinner!!

I forgot to mention that yesterday morning we met a hiker coming towards us wearing hiking boots, gaiters, and a nice jacket. He stopped to chat with us. Bob is through-hiking (sort of) the entire trail, but heading the opposite direction (south to north). Yesterday was his fifteenth(?) day of hiking. He's keeping a blog and took our picture for today's posting. The blog is called "Robert's Adventure" or something like that. Leslie is going to look for it. Super nice guy. He's from Swansea and he said that he's intermixing hiking one-day sections of the trail with spending time at work. So far, his dad has been picking him up at the end of the day and driving him back to his apartment. So, he's definitely taking days off in between his walking days. That's why I wrote that he was "sort of" through-hiking the trail. He said he's planning to finish this year, so in that sense he's finishing the trail in one year. Bob is only the second through-hiker we've met besides our German friend, Nicole.

Leslie's Journal Entry:

OMG. Our mini apartment is so cute! Pizza place across the street. Bakery around the corner. No heat, and the apartment is freezing. But you can't have everything.

Friday, October 20, 2017, Hiking Day 60!!
3-miles before Burry Port to Loughor – 14 miles
13 miles; Total – 699½ miles

It is late. My belly is full of a fab meal and dessert, and its 8:30pm and almost time for bed. So, I'm not really in the mood to write much. We are getting into more populated and industrial parts of southern Wales and I think it will get even more so as we near the cities of Swansea and Cardith, and eventually Chepstow.

Today's 14 miles were almost entirely on paved or gravel cycle paths, sidewalks, and old abandoned tarmac roads. Easy and fast walking, but hard on my feet and ankles. The little bones in my left foot especially ached today. Almost like little stress fractures. I tried walking in the grass along the side of the paved cycleway as much as possible.

The sun came in and out all day. Chill when it went behind the clouds, but perfect for walking when it came out. The temperature was around 56 degrees. Only eleven days to November! Tomorrow's weather is a bit depressing. The forecast is for 40mph winds, gusting to 50 and 60mph! And rain all day long. So, we are preparing mentally for a long, wet, windy, chilly day. The high is supposed to be around 55 degrees, but with stiff wind and rain it'll be cold. It's times like these, and lots of other times, that I'm happy we have a warm, dry place to sleep every night on this trip.

I'm planning to start out in my rain pants. I'll be wearing them for the first time on our trip. On Day 61! I think I'm also going to hike with my fleece jacket under my raincoat. Another first. It'll be too hot, but I'm planning to be soaked, so I'd rather be wet and warm, than wet and chilled.

We pass through a couple of small villages tomorrow, so hopefully we can find some spots to get out of the wind and rain for a bit.

We LOVE the place we've been staying these past two nights. The Witford. We are in a mini apartment that is super cute. We just had a great dinner downstairs in their restaurant. And they offered us two free desserts because the heat in our room is screwed up. We got a slice of peanut butter and chocolate cheesecake, and a piece of apple rhubarb crumble. I'm overly stuffed, and sleepy.

Leslie's Journal Entry:

It really hurts to sit, bare-assed, in nettles. I know this because I accidentally squatted to pee in them today.

Pretty crisp fall-like walk today. Hurricane expected tomorrow. I am fighting off depression. Jon says he is just not thinking about it, but he keeps checking the weather. I prayed out loud about it today. I have not prayed since I was 10 and really wanted a tape recorder for Christmas. Jon crossed his fingers. He said that if between these two things, the weather does not change, then there is no God.

Saturday, October 21, 2017, Hiking Day 61
Loughor to Llanmadoc – 13 miles
Total – 712½ miles

We hit the 700-mile mark a few seconds after we started walking this morning!! It's weird. The first few hundred-mile marks seemed like such major milestones that we anticipated and sort of celebrated in our own way. The last couple, the 600-mile mark and the 700-

mile mark, just sort of came and went with little fanfare. I think we are both just anxious to be done, and the final goal, the endpoint, has been our focus now for a while so these intermediate goals are less meaningful. And after two months, walking is just what we do every day. We get up and we walk.

We've successfully cut off one full day of hiking by adding more miles the last four days, and tomorrow we'll start chipping away at cutting off a second full day.

We agonized last night about today's weather forecast, but it wasn't as bad as we'd both dreaded and had been mentally prepared for. It did blow a constant 40mph all day, and there were definitely gusts of wind that stopped us in our tracks or made it seem like we were walking in slow motion for a few steps. And when it did rain hard, the rain came at us sideways and stung our bare skin like needles. But, thankfully, the rains only lasted a few minutes each time they passed through, and we stayed on the cycleways and then roads the entire time and were shielded from a lot of the wind by high hedges and occasional stone walls.

I wore my rain pants for the first time of the entire trip . . . all day. And we both wore our fleece jackets a good part of the day, too, underneath our raincoats. So, it was a constant clothes shuffle of putting fleece hat on, taking hats off for Leslie; and for me, baseball cap on (to keep the rain off my face), and baseball cap off; fleece jackets on to keep from getting too chilled, and fleece jackets off to keep from getting too sweaty.

We only stopped twice all day. Once very briefly, during a driving rain, we stopped under a little covered bus shelter to put our fleece on, and then a second time for lunch at the Greyhound Pub to get out of the weather and warm up by their wood stove fire.

We're staying at the Forge Cottage B&B in Llanmadoc, run by Pearl and Mike and their dog, Bella. Pearl is an older lady who was super cute. She offered to do a load of laundry, which was only the third time someone has offered. She also took our wet coats and rain pants and hung them in the breakfast room today, and gave me newspaper to stuff in our soaked hiking shoes. Leslie said that Pearl reminded us of Juanita, my neighbor in Kasaan, Alaska, who was crusty and harsh on the outside, but sweet and friendly on the inside.

We're both feeling that the end of this adventure is near. I'm starting to make lists of work things I need to do as soon as I get home, as well as home chores that will need my attention. I'm making travel plans to Washington, D.C., and Alaska. Leslie is working on our family Thanksgiving plans to head up to Minnesota. It's becoming harder and harder to stay focused on what we still need to do here in Wales. And crappy weather days like today simply aren't fun. It just feels like a job that needs to be completed. During a 75-day hike, some days are just like that.

Leslie's Journal Entry:

There is no God.

Sunday, October 22, 2017, Hiking Day 62
Llanmadoc to Rhossili to 3-miles the Worm's Head Hotel
11 miles; Total – 723½ miles

This journal entry is going to sound negative. We are sitting in the pub at the Worm's Head Hotel in amazingly beautiful Rhossili on the end of Gower Peninsula. It really is stunning, and our little table is by a window looking out over the sea. It is storming outside and cozy and warm inside. We hiked eight miles from our Forge Cottage B&B in Llanmadoc to Rhossili, and then we walked another three miles to get a few more out of the way. Enough of the positive and on to the negative.

1. There is a couple sitting at a table a few feet away from us, probably in their late 50s or early 60s. The lady (who looks a lot like my brother Steve) is basically having sex with the guy she is with. Super annoying. A little too intimate for a public restaurant.

2. The owner of the "family run" Worm's Head Hotel met us as we walked into the bar, and as soon as he found out we were from the States, launched into how much greater the U.S. is now that Trump is president. My heart hasn't raced that fast in a long time. I was seconds away from launching into a tirade about what a fuck-hole Trump is when Leslie poked me in the ribs, which is the universal signal for, "Let's get the hell out of here." So, I abruptly asked him some questions about getting food in the bar, and we left.

3. I just wrote a Trip Advisor review for the Worm's Head Hotel. It included the fact that it was 49 degrees outside this morning and got to a high of 54 degrees, and when we got to our room at 2:15pm it was freezing and the radiator heat was turned off. I went out to the front desk and asked about the heat in our room, and the receptionist said, "Yes, I thought it felt cold when we showed you to your room. But I'm sorry. The heat won't come on until 4pm." Mind you, it was 50 degrees outside. The shower literally had black mold growing in the cracks of the tiles, and the soap dish was all rusty. The shower drain didn't drain property, so my shower was completed while wading in ankle-deep water. And this $125/night room that advertised that it had internet apparently only has a signal in the lobby that has no chairs, and in the dank, dark, creepy T.V. lounge.

4. We arrived at the Worm's Head Hotel at 1:45pm and the receptionist told us that our room wasn't ready, and that we should come back "a little before 2pm." Isn't 1:45pm already a little before 2pm? We literally left, came back five minutes later, and our room was ready.

5. When we got to our room, the coffee service had two little pack-

ets of instant coffee for two people. Two little dinky packets. So, I went to the receptionist and politely asked for more coffee packets and they brought 10 creamers, six decaf packets, and two more little packets of regular coffee.

6. I ordered five-bean chili for dinner at the hotel restaurant, and I swear to God there wasn't even five beans total in the chili. And it was served with rice. WTF? Get me outta this Worm's Head hell-hole.

In re-reading this entry, it sounds petty. But I think that after hiking for 62 days, and always looking forward to stopping, relaxing, warming up, and eating a good meal, this place was just a disappointment from top to bottom. Especially for $125.

Leslie's Journal Entry:

So, we are sitting in a bar having a needed drink after the old, fat, white owner of our hotel just went on about how great Trump is. I saw the hair on Jon's back go up like a cat, so I pinched him under the table, and we just talked about the stupid idiot behind his back.

I wanted to say, "Can I grab you by your pussy, since you obviously have one? Oh, and your showers are dirty with black mold in the cracks. And we have not been here but a few hours and have already written a scathing review on Yelp. So, HA!" But I didn't.

I just read part of the bar menu to Jon.

Me: *Slow-cooked ox cheek?*

Jon: *Yeah, you don't want to cook that too fast.*

Monday, October 23, 2017, Hiking Day 63
Rhossili to Oxwich
11 miles; Total – 734½ miles

My highlight for today was meeting John in the village of Horton. We'd hiked seven and a half or so miles from where we'd ended yesterday in a heavy fog and occasional rain. I was pretty soaked. We'd just stopped for a mediocre lunch at a little shop above the beach in the village of Eynon, which Leslie called "Eeyore" throughout the day. I was just happy that something was open for lunch since we weren't carrying any lunch with us today. We both got a "salad sandwich," which was a chicken breast with lettuce and tomato. A little bit of a misnomer. At this tiny little café, they insisted on keeping the front door open, even after I asked if we could close it. So, we tried to sit around the corner out of the direct wind coming in the door from the 50-degree day. I also had a little fish cake, which wasn't too bad.

Anyway, we walked along the beaches through "Eeyore" and then on through a little 10-horse village known as Horton. (No, we didn't hear a "who.") There were two guys standing outside a house. One guy looked like a construction worker, and the other guy was named John. We chatted a minute about the weather and about our hike, and the construction worker said he had to go, and warned me with a wink, that we'd better start walking or John would stand and talk to us for the rest of the day. John immediately invited us in for "Coffee? Tea? To use the loo?" He was desperate to get us to stay and chat.

I got the feeling that everyone in the area knows John. He looked like an old burned-out rocker with four earrings in each ear, long, greying and unkempt hair, and a pair of women's slip-on shoes on his feet. At one point, when he told us he had to show us his garden, he said, "Oh, I'm not wearing the right shoes for this," as we walked through tall, wet grass. We heard about his recently deceased Czech wife, and the history of the large but seemingly uncared for six-bedroom house we were standing in front of.

John invited us in again, several more times actually, but Leslie and I both knew that once we went in his house for coffee, we'd never get out. He told us that when he traveled in Northern Scotland, the locals were so starved for human contact that they'd almost force visitors to come in for tea or a drink. Anyway, John's friendliness and hospitality were the highlight of this otherwise wet and dreary day.

The guidebook for today's section reads, "This part of the Gower Peninsula contains some of the finest sections of coastal walking in the country." We walked through dense fog the entire day. The kind of dense fog where we could only see 15 or 20 feet in front of us. The same thing happened to us when we hiked out of Holy Head on the Isle of Anglesey, again one of the most stunning sections of the trail. We hiked that entire day in total mist and heavy fog as well.

The last four and a half miles or so was a complete mud-fest. Literally every step on the trail was through slippery mud or puddles or both. Leslie slipped and fell flat on her ass once, which makes it four to zero in terms of complete falls to the ground while hiking. I credit my lead in this competition to the fact that I'm a two-poler, and Leslie is only a one-poler.

We also met "Evo" on the trial today. He's a middle-aged Canadian who is doing a few day hikes in the area before heading to a three-week yoga retreat in the hill country of India, and then on to three more weeks of volunteering in Sri Lanka. Sounds really interesting. He'd started in Horton this morning and was heading to Rhossili in the rain and fog.

We're staying at the Oxwich Bay Hotel tonight in their "Ivy Cottage" in a really nice room. The hotel also has a great restaurant and a little bar area. And the room is the cheapest we've stayed in in weeks. I wish we could stay here for another night. Tomorrow we are going to start adding miles every day for the next four days to pick up one more day in our schedule so that we can finish on November 2nd, and hopefully fly home on November 3rd. So, instead of going the nine miles tomorrow that the guidebook suggests, I want to go 13. Both of our bodies are feeling the aches and pains of hiking for 63 straight days.

Leslie's Journal Entry:

Tuesday, October 24, 2017, Hiking Day 64
Oxwich Bay to Caswell Bay – 9 miles
Caswell Bay to the Mumbles (Oystermouth Castle) – 4 miles
13 miles; Total – 747½ miles

Today was a bit tougher than I'd expected. There were a lot more ups and downs, and it basically rained all day long. A lot of the day it was just this heavy, misty rain, but it soaked us nonetheless. I was pretty well soaked to the skin after an hour of hiking, first along the beach at Oxwich Bay and then through the sand dunes and up into the high bluffs.

We missed much of the scenery due to heavy fog again today. But, despite the rain and the wind, there were definitely a few highlights that got us through.

About two hours into the hike, the trail dropped down into a wide bay with a river running through the middle. The crossing was on huge stone blocks that were each 12 to 24 inches underwater when we got there. So, after standing there for a few minutes trying to figure out if we had any other options, we took off our shoes and socks, tied the shoes together and flung them over our shoulder, loosed our backpack waist belts in case we fell over and needed to get out of our packs quickly, and then forged across the river through very cold water in our bare feet. The river was about three feet deep or so, so balancing on each stone block was important.

Part way across I realized that standing on the other side taking pictures of us was our buddy Evo from the other day. He was out in the rain as well for another one of his short day hikes. It was great to see a familiar face. He sent us the photos he took later in the day.

After another hour or so hiking in the rain, we were so happy to happen upon a really cute little coffee shop in a village that had nothing but the little coffee shop. It had sort of just appeared out of the fog. I had just finished saying to Leslie that we needed to be careful in this thick fog that we didn't get turned around or lost. Both of us were soaked, so it was a little embarrassing being among normal dry people in the coffee shop.

We set down our wet packs, and took off our wet raincoats, and had some great coffee! Leslie had a vegan chocolate chip cookie, and I had a piece of quiche. The whole while, two nicely dressed older ladies were sitting at the next table and watching us closely. As we got up to leave, one of them started asking us questions about what and where and why. One of the ladies said, "I can't wait to tell my husband about this."

The concept of hiking for 64 straight days is pretty foreign to most people. And as they watched us put back on our soaking wet stuff and head back out into the wind and rain and fog, they seemed pretty amazed. They said several times, "You must be in good shape." Afterwards, Leslie said that it almost feels like it minimizes the challenge of what we're doing day in and day out by people saying, "Oh, you must be in such good shape." We're actually in our 50s, and in average shape. And every day, after 64 days, it is still hard to get up and keep going every day.

Today we walked four miles beyond the guidebook suggested destination for today in Caswell Bay so that we could get a head start on making up one more day. One cool thing in Caswell Bay was seeing a big mansion up above the beach with a private helicopter parked in the front yard!!

Tonight, we're staying in a fancy hotel in downtown Swansea called the Morgan Hotel. Very old and grandiose. After a long cold hike, we decided to just have dinner at the hotel. So, after amazing hot showers, we had a couple of gourmet cheese plates with crackers and some mixed drinks. And then hobbled back to our room for the night.

Leslie's Journal Entry:

This morning Jon needed to use the bathroom while we waited for the taxi, so he ran back inside the hotel. When he came out he said, "I had a little trouble finding the bathroom." He apparently went to the first door labeled with an "M" and could not get in. He went to a second door labeled with an "M" and could not get in. Then he realized we were staying at the Morgan Hotel and every door was labeled with an "M."

We walked 17 miles today. No way to make that not sound sick. Especially when it was supposed to be 16 but we had to backtrack to McDonald's to retrieve Jon's wallet.

Wednesday, October 25, 2017, Hiking Day 65
Mumbles to Swansea– 5 miles
Swansea to Port Talbot – 11 miles
Lost wallet – 1 mile
17 miles; Total – 764½ miles

We spent a second night at the fancy Hotel Morgan, so we only had day packs on today. It's always a nice treat to hike for a day without our full backpacks. Today we started the first section of our final trail guidebook. There are seven guidebooks for this Wales Coast Path and we just started the seventh and final section from Swansea to Chepstow. It feels like a milestone to both of us.

We caught a taxi back to where we ended yesterday at the co-op grocery store in Mumbles/Oyster Bay and followed a really nice paved cycle-way around Swansea Bay to the town of Swansea.

Our plan was to go the five miles into downtown Swansea, and then another eight miles or so out the other side, which would leave a 15-and-a-half-mile day tomorrow with our big packs on so we could pick up that second day. But, once we got walking this morning, the sun was actually out for the first time in days, so we decided early on that we would walk all the way to Port Talbot today for a total of 16 miles just to get more miles out of the way on such a nice day. And the "I lost my wallet" debacle added another mile for a total of 17 miles today! Oh, my aching feet.

It was a long day of around seven hours of walking, but overall it went well and we were really happy afterwards that we went the extra few miles. It is the first day that I've hiked in a T-shirt and sunglasses in quite a while. (I wore shorts and socks, too.)

This morning we had a nice complimentary breakfast at the Morgan Hotel. A too-fancy place for us, in our hiking shorts and T-shirts. After breakfast, we waited for a taxi to take us back to the Oyster Bay co-op. I had to pee, so I wandered around the lobby of the hotel and saw a door with an "M" on it, but it was locked. I went into the bar area and saw two more doors with an "M" on them, but they were locked, too. I was about to pee my pants when I realized that pretty much every door had an "M" imprinted on it, and then saw tons of "M"s on the carpet. It took me a bit to realize that "M" stood for Morgan, not the Men's Room.

The highlight and the lowlight of the day was stopping for a late lunch at McDonald's on the outskirts of Port Talbot, about 11 miles into our day. Our second McDonalds of the trip, and we were pretty excited. We both got quarter-pounders and fries, and split a chocolate milkshake, just like in the good 'ol days when we were young and skinny. About a half-mile after leaving McDonalds, all fat and happy, I realized I didn't have my billfold. Idiot. We raced back, not sure if it was worse to lose my wallet or that we were backtracking and adding an extra mile to our day. I was pretty sure I must have swept it into the garbage along with everything else on my tray.

Thankfully, the lady sweeping the floor had found it on the floor by our table! All was well!! That's the second time I've lost my wallet on this trip.

Our now 17 miles finished along a nice beach-front path heading towards Port Talbot. And the section for today literally ended at a non-descript roundabout. Weird.

Leslie's Journal Entry:

SECTION SEVEN:
SOUTH WALES COAST

Swansea to Chepstow

Thursday, October 26, 2017, Hiking Day 66
Port Talbot to Porthcawl – 11½ miles
Total – 766 miles

We develop morning and evening routines after traveling for 66 straight days. When we first get to the room where we're staying for the night, we both unpack everything from our backpacks. Coats get hung up; wet clothes (socks and shoes especially) are draped over a heater and shoes are stuffed with newspaper; post-shower clothes are set out; toiletry bags are placed in the bathroom; books, journals, and reading glasses are set on the bedside stand; power cords for phone, computer, and iPad are plugged in. I also set out my notepad that lists the "office" work I need to get done.

Everything else comes out of the pack and goes in an orderly pile in a corner of the room. We also decide when we first walk into the room who gets what space to unpack. Leslie hates a room that looks disorganized, so if the room has a dresser, closet, or armoire, she always gets it, and puts her things away and out of sight. I also always need a flat place, like a desk or table, to set out my phone, loose change, guidebook and map, wallet, sunglasses, hat, and anything that is hanging around in my pockets.

It all sounds very anal as I'm writing it down, but moving to a new place almost every night and sharing a small space day after day, this routine has probably eliminated countless arguments. And, the routines help provide a little predictable order in what otherwise is constantly changing every day.

Mornings also have a route, but in reverse. I typically get up around 6:30am. Leslie has been enjoying waking up early and having an hour and a half or so to ease into the day, so she's been getting up early, too. I heat a pot of water in the electric hot water pot that is always in every room. I make two cups of instant coffee, putting in two instant coffee packets into each cup so that it's good and strong, with a little sugar in Leslie's. We lay in bed, check emails, the weather, and news headlines. And then try to get some work done.

It really only takes 15 minutes to completely pack up, and we almost always have our complimentary breakfast at 8:30am. Sometimes at 8:15am. We bring our packed-up backpacks to the breakfast area, and leave as soon as we're done eating.

Every day. Just like that.

Leslie's Journal Entry:

So . . . butterflies are lovely but one must draw a line between a tasteful amount of butterflies when your B&B is called The Butterfly Guesthouse and having so many butterflies that it is creepy. This one is on the creepy end of the butterfly scale.

Friday, October 27, 2017, Hiking Day 67
Porthcawl to Ogmore-By-Sea – 9 miles
Ogmore to Dunraven Bay (Dunraven Castle) – 3 miles
Total – 788 miles

Yesterday's hike of 12 miles seemed longer and harder than it should have been. It was misty and rainy for most of the day. We walked past lots of industrial areas—a steel mill and other massive smokey factories. And we were especially tired after walking 16 miles the day before. Last night we stayed at the Butterfly Guest House. Butterfly shit everywhere. Wall hangings, bedspreads, soap dishes. Everywhere you looked.

For dinner last night we ate at a small place on the waterfront called The Cozy Corner. We were pleasantly surprised to find that they had several French dishes. I ended up getting mussels in an amazing red sauce with spicy sausages, and even better carrot soup. Leslie got a seafood stew that was mind blowing. A great find. Great food. And all for 39£.

Today's hike seemed to fly by, even though it was 12 miles. It had everything to do with the weather. Sunny all day long! Even though the high was only 58 degrees, it felt hot, more like mid to high 70s. We did some beach walking, estuary walking, and a river crossing on partially submerged stone blocks (resulting in soakers), had lunch on a park bench above the beach in Ogmore-By-Sea, and walked the last three miles to Dunraven Bay. We had a taxi called and were in our room at a Best Western in the nearby town of Bridgend by 3:30pm!! A really great day.

Now for a pint of Welsh cider (Pinot Grigio for Leslie) and some dinner.

Leslie's Journal Entry:

After breakfast, we walked to a grocery to buy something for lunch. We stopped at a bathroom and Jon took forever.

When he came out, he said, "I had a situation."

Me: *Yea?*

Jon: *Walk. . . . We need to be out of earshot of other people.*

Me: *Tell me!*

Jon: *I thought I crapped my pants, but it ended up just being a multiple wipe situation.*

Me: *That's it?*

Saturday, October 28, 2017, Hiking Day 68
Dunraven Bay to a car park by W. Aberthaw – 12 miles
Total – 800 miles!!!!

800 miles on the dot! Amazing!!! We, of course, haven't counted all the walking to and from restaurants and grocery stores, etc. once we finish our hiking for the day. But according to my daily tabulations, we hit our 800-mile mark as we reached the gravel car park, literally feet away from a massive power plant that we'd been staring at off in the distance for the last four miles of the hike.

While we waited for a taxi, Leslie painted "800 Miles" on a round smooth beach rock with red fingernail polish. And then we proceeded to take several photos with the rock, and Monkey Face, and ourselves with the rock and Monkey Face. Now it feels like we are close to the end of this adventure. Less than a week to go, and fewer than 100 miles!!

A few times yesterday and today I've made a point of just looking around as I walk and consciously thinking about what a great trip this has been, and how nice it is to be walking along the coast of Wales with my backpack on, getting some exercise, sharing this experience with Leslie, and just being outside. In a few short days, I'll be back home and this trip and these moments will feel like they took place years ago. Normal day-to-day life will resume all too quickly.

The 12-mile hike today was mostly on bluffs sitting high above the sea. The 250-foot-high cliffs are made of hundreds of layers of sediment and apparently contain 350-million-year-old fossils. We passed some several thousand-year-old Iron Age fort mounts, and more recent 400- to 500-year-old castle remnants, and then past several Second World War fortifications and concrete barriers constructed to repel a tank invasion that would be mounted by sea. Millenia of fortifications built to protect the land and the people.

Our Best Western pre-packed lunch wasn't that great. And we ate it at a picnic table by the parking area and beach at Llantwit Major. But it was windy and cold and so we ate quickly so we could keep moving and stay warm.

What we are doing is lost on most people. Sometimes people, like the ones at the beach picnic spot today or at a B&B, will ask what we're doing. Yesterday I told a woman that we've hiked around the entire coast of Wales, and she replied, "Oh, have you walked in the Gowers? It's so lovely there." I was like, "Yeah, we hiked through the Gowers a few days ago (after we'd already hiked 700 miles)." Today an older lady in a restroom asked Leslie if she had been camping along the way since she noticed we had such big back-packs. When Leslie said no, the lady sort of lost interest, like, "Oh, since you're not camping, what's the big deal?"

I don't blame people (too much, anyway). Most people have no point of comparison for doing a 10-week, 870-mile hike. It's just not something they can relate to. When we say we've been walking every day since the last week of August, and this being the end of October, people's eyes seem to open a bit wider.

Tomorrow is Leslie's 54th birthday. We are staying at a nice Marriott Hotel in the center of Cardiff. I'm hoping we'll find a sushi restaurant there for dinner tomorrow night. I've ordered her a couple of things online that she'll hopefully get an email about tomorrow, and I created a funny e-birthday card that should get delivered in an email on her birthday, too. It's hard to do things for her birthday while we're hiking. But if I can find sushi and some chocolate birthday cake, she'll be happy!

Leslie's Journal Entry:

Jon likes it when he looks over and I'm writing in my journal. He wants me to contribute. I look over at him and he is writing pages and pages full of wonderful details so that we will never forget this amazing trip.

But the truth is, I don't want to write tonight. What could I possibly say that he hasn't already written about in detail?

All I remember is that it was flat-ish, and my feet hurt. And tomorrow I am 54 freaking years old and if I don't want to write, I don't have to. I need time to meditate on my old age.

Sunday, October 29, 2017, Hiking Day 69
W. Aberthaw Car Park to Barry Island – 8 miles
Barry Island to Cardoxon Train Station – 4 miles
Total – 812 miles

Leslie's Birthday Extravaganza started with an electronic gift card from Bare Necessities; and then an email with the eleven best-selling books of 2017 that I had delivered to our house; followed by a funny Jib-Jab e-card that featured me, Seth, Tyler, and my dad dancing to some funny song. Her amazing birthday ended with a stay at the Cardiff Marriott, a fancy drink in the Marriott lounge, and dinner at a nearby Thai restaurant. It wasn't the best birthday she's ever had, but not bad for trying to pull something together while on a 870-mile hike.

Other than all that, it was kind of a boring day of a lot of urban walking. We started by walking around a huge coal-fired power plant. Early on, we made a bad choice by choosing to walk along the shingle (rocky) seashore, rather than hiking up onto some bluffs. We shuffled and wobbled over the shoreline of rounded, loose rocks for 10 minutes or so only to get to a spot where we couldn't continue because the tide was too high. So, we had to turn around and backtrack, which we hate(!!!) on loose beach rock that Leslie really hates walking on. Win some. Lose some.

For the rest of the morning, the trail went through two caravan parks; across a big grassy lot that was preparing for a "boot sale" (like a flea market where people drive up and sell shit out of the trunk of their car); within a half-mile of the big Cardiff International Airport; and then along the little causeway that connects Barry Island with the city of Barry. Barry Island, which isn't an island anymore, is an aging amusement park. It looked pretty rusty and run down to me. But it is a Sunday and a beautiful sunny Sunday at that, so there were lots of families and couples-in-love that were milling around.

After getting some lunch, we took an "official" shortcut around the island, and then walked our final three or four miles through Barry to get to the Cardoxon Train Station. I'm never sure which side of the tracks to stand on to catch the train that is heading in the direction that we want to go, or how to read the train schedule. But right away, a young teenaged boy, who was leaning against his bicycle and smoking a cigarette, noticed my confusion and offered to help us figure out which train, which direction, and which stop to get off at. Another more homeless-looking guy came over pushing his bicycle and chimed in with his helpful advice. Super nice!!

We both love riding on the trains in Wales. For a few minutes, we don't have to walk and can just sit and look out the windows at the scenery that we've been walking through for months. The ticket-taker guys are always nice and helpful, too. We got off at the Cardiff Central Station and asked directions to the Marriott, which was only a block or so away.

I'm sure we looked out of place in the fancy hotel lobby and lounge with our dirty backpacks, and me in my faded short pants. But, hey, it's Leslie's Birthday!!

Leslie's Journal Entry:

Happy Birthday to me!

To celebrate, we walked 14 miles.

Then we went to dinner and had brownies and ice cream and Jon, as always, was a generous gift giver.

Tomorrow is still my birthday, according to me, and we've decided to walk again! What?

Monday, October 30, 2017, Hiking Day 70
Cardoxon Train Station to Barry – 10 miles
Barry to Cardiff Barrage – 5 miles
Total – 827 miles

This morning we were both wide awake at 5:45am. Weird for me. Really weird for Leslie. I walked to a nearby Starbucks at 6:30am and came back to our room with two amazing cups of coffee with extra shots of espresso to toughen them up. No decent breakfast sandwiches, but some yummy pumpkin bread and a muffin.

We dropped some dirty laundry off at the front desk of the Marriott and walked to the Cardiff Center train station that is right next to a huge, new 70,000-fan rugby stadium. We caught the train back to the Cadoxon Station.

Today's 15-mile hike was partly through towns and partly along paths and sidewalks that ran along the coast. It was only 48 degrees when we started out and for most of the morning it was pretty chilly walking along the shady route. Leslie wore her new down jacket for the entire morning, and I hiked in my fleece jacket for the first time this trip. I actually wore it for most of the day, along with my shorts.

We stopped in the cute little coastal town of Penarth for an early light lunch. Because of the cold, we walked fast and had 15 miles completed by around 2:30pm!! Part of the route brought us right back into the center of Cardiff and through a really cool, revitalized industrial and port area. There was lots of greenspace, parks, a huge skatepark, people walking their dogs, and families out for a walk. And it was a nice sunny day, so a beautiful day for a walk.

We passed an exhibition and a cool statue that commemorated the 100th anniversary of the Robert Falcon Scott Antarctic expedition. We actually took the time to read a brief history of that fateful expedition. Scott and his crew departed from Cardiff. His First Officer was from Cardiff and one of his crew was from the Gowar Peninsula.

We caught a taxi back from our 15-mile stopping point and were sitting in the Prince of Wales Pub drinking an IPA by 3:30pm!! Now that's a great Wales Coast Path hiking day!!

Shower, sushi dinner, and back in our room by 7pm reading the latest news on the indictment of Paul Manafort that was unsealed this morning. We are both so hoping that this is just the first of many in Trump's inner circle who are going down, and who will hopefully take Trump down with them!!

Only three more days of hiking to go. It's hard to believe that we are so close to being done. It seems like we started a lifetime ago.

Leslie's Journal Entry:

Fifteen-mile walk today, but it went fast because it was sunny and went partly through a town.

We ate Japanese for dinner, which included green beans and chicken in miso sauce, and sweet corn and pickles that tasted like turpentine.

The good news is Robert Muller just indicted some of Trump's peeps in the Russian probe.

Tuesday, October 31, 2017, Hiking Day 71
Corner of Rover Way & Darbi to Newport – 14 miles
Total – 841 miles

We are staying in a really cool place tonight: The Waterloo Hotel and Bistro. It is an old historic hotel that probably had its heyday in the early 1900s. It is directly across the street from a very unusual suspension bridge, The Newport Transporter Bridge, one of only 21 of its kind ever built. It was opened in 1906 and is considered "one of the Wonders of Wales." This is a bridge that raises (the entire bridge) up and down to account for a 47-foot tidal change to allow ships to pass underneath.

Anyway, the Waterloo was probably built when that bridge opened. It has a big bar and restaurant downstairs that feels like you're still in the early 1900s. The rooms have been completely updated and are nice, with super high ceilings. And very tall windows. The restaurant has a couple of chefs and the items on the menu are super fancy and kind of expensive. We didn't know what half of the things even were. But we went down at 5:30pm and had wine and cider and then some really great food.

The sad thing is that there was hardly anyone in the restaurant, and I don't think anyone else is staying in the hotel. As we finished our hike here today, we saw that the Waterloo was located in a run-down part of Newport. So, the whole place and setting has sort of a sad feel to it.

We hiked 14 miles today, from the east side of the city of Cardiff into the city of Newport. A lot of the hiking was past a huge, noisy steel plant and a stinky landfill, and then a power plant and some other garbagy rundown area. There was a six-mile stretch that ran along a raised earthen causeway, but you could see the industries in the distance and it ended up just being a long, boring stretch.

Two highlights, in addition to dinner at the Waterloo:

1) After a few miles, we passed an older couple sitting on a bench. The guy had been literally staring at us as we approached. They were hiking the entire Wales Coast Path in day-hike sections. A day here and a day there. I think they've been plugging away at it for the past few years. They actually live in Cardiff and were very interested in this being our 71st day with only two days to go after today. They asked us lots of questions and several times, the guy said things like, "That's so great! You guys are doing a great job! Nice work. What an accomplishment."

As we parted ways, I said to Leslie that it is so rare to run into people who have a real grasp of what it is that we're doing, and what an accomplishment it really is. These people understood, and they were full of congratulations. It's starting to sink in a little that we're on the verge of completing a pretty big accomplishment. The woman also showed us a photo she had on her phone of what marks the finish of the 870-mile trail in Chepstow, so we have a visual image of the actual end point.

2) About four miles from the end today, a trail sign pointed towards an old grassy farm road, but there was a locked gate in the way, which was a little odd. There were Wales Coast Path signs pointing in both directions, but the locked gate felt a little weird. So, we climbed over the top of the gate and kept walking. About a mile later, there was another farm gate that was also locked, so we climbed over that one, too. I felt that something odd was going on, like the farmer (it was a huge dairy farm) had rescinded permission for hikers to cross his pasture.

As we walked down a dirt road leading away from the entrance to the farm, we started passing several signs that said things like, "No Trespassing" and "Trespassers Will be Prosecuted," and even a few "This Property is Monitored by Closed Circuit T.V." Oopps.

Two farmers drove past us on their tractors, and neither seemed very friendly. It wasn't until we were off the farm road and back on public property that we saw some kind of trail diversion sign and realized that our three- or four-year-old guidebook must not have included a more recent trail change. There is a Wales Coast Path phone app and website that includes trail updates, but we haven't ever checked it in 71 days. So why start now?

Leslie's Journal Entry:

Happy Halloween!

We are dressed like hikers with sore feet for Halloween and are really looking the part!

It was an ugly day walking through an industrial area, smelling stinky chemicals, and walking through cow shit. But . . . I don't care because we go home in just three days. It feels surreal. I'm so excited. Jon probably wrote about how sad he is.

Wednesday, November 1, 2017, Hiking Day 72
Newport (Waterloo Hotel) to Redwick – 14 miles
Total – 855 miles

I can't believe it's November! We started hiking on August 22nd and now it's November!! We spent a lot of time today talking about the feelings that go along with knowing that tomorrow afternoon we are done! It feels like we've been walking and staying in B&Bs and hotels forever. On one hand, we are both really looking forward to getting home. We each have so much to do workwise. It'll be nice to just get home and start chipping away at the lists I've been creating.

A few weeks ago, it seemed like we still had so many more days and weeks to go. And now we're on the verge of being done. And we both know that the second we get home it'll feel like we never left. The trip will just be hundreds and thousands of little memories. And I know that within days I'll start making plans for my next two or three adventures for 2018. Maybe Brazil to climb Pico da Neblina; maybe hiking the longest trail in South Korea, the Baek-du-Daegan Trail; maybe a canoe trip; definitely another international trip with Leslie. Who knows?

We've both had this weird reoccurring experience over the last few weeks. Yesterday, when we were likely trespassing through a farmer's field, we were approaching some dirty and mangy horses and I said out loud, "I wonder why farmers have horses like these. They aren't groomed or brushed. And it doesn't look like they are for riding." And Leslie said, "I was just thinking that exact same thing." Weird.

This seems to be happening daily now, or even more than once a day. We'll be walking and not talking for long periods of time, like an hour, and one of us will say something and it is literally what the other person was about to say at that exact same moment. I know it is not a coincidence because it's happening a lot. But, after being side-by-side virtually 24 hours every day for the last 75 straight days, our thoughts are really in synch. We're experiencing the same things, and perceiving them the same way in many cases, which is then causing the same thoughts or utterances. Or maybe it's just love!

We decided to take a chance and not bring any lunch food with us today. Just some snacks.

But the pub we passed around mile 10 ended up not opening until 4pm. Oops. It was the only store or eating placed we passed all day. But as our trail headed back to the shoreline, we neared a small tea shop that the guidebook says is only open in the summer, and it was open! So, we sat at a picnic table and had sandwiches and chips and pop, served by the nicest lady and her young granddaughter. (Kids in Wales are all off school this week.). The lady even brought us a couple of complimentary "Welsh Cakes." So, we found some food after all.

My right foot is starting to give me some problems. It just aches after only a short period of walking. It's like the bones and joints around my big toe, and that part of my foot, are bruised or arthritic. I think it's mostly because I've now hiked about 1,000 miles in these shoes and they are starting to break down. One more day and I'm dumping them in the trash. They are completely falling apart, and they stink horribly. I can't wait to drop them in the garbage the second we reach the end of the trail tomorrow!!

Leslie's Journal Entry:

Today was another walk that wasn't so pretty, but I had a spring in my step because we have one more day after today. I feel like I don't even remember home. I have woken up so many mornings asking, "Where are we?" because we have been so many places.

I am proud of us. Not so much for the physical feat, but for our mental stamina to do this every freaking day for 73 days without one day off.

Why, if I can do this, can't I do 10 minutes of sit ups?

Thursday, November 2, 2017, Hiking Day 73
Redwick to Chepstow – 14½ miles
Total – 869½ miles!!!!!

Last Day!!!!

We're drinking gin and tonics on the train back to Paddington Station in London. This train really knows how to help us celebrate our success. For both of us, the idea of hiking for 73 straight days, and traveling 870 miles, was really just a series of stringing one day after another together. Seventy-three day hikes, some harder and more challenging than others. But that's how we've handled this entire adventure. Just getting up every morning. Packing our backpacks, and then walking for most of the day, and feeling good about the day's accomplishment. The impressiveness of hiking 870 miles is lost on most people, and it is really sort of lost on me, too. But, after we got to the final marker in Chepstow, and the end (or the beginning) of the Wales Coast Path, we sent out photos to our fan club of family members. Anna wrote back, "Bad Asses!" We called our kids, Seth and Tyler, and both of them seemed to really appreciate the magnitude of what we just accomplished.

As we were standing there at the end, sort of wondering what to do next now that our hike was finished, an older guy came up to us and said, "Are you planning to hike the Wales Coast Path?" (He'd noticed our backpacks.) We both replied in unison and said, "No, we just finished hiking the entire path." His jaw sort of dropped and he gave Leslie a hug and shook my hand, and said, "Congratulations. That's quite an accomplishment. Amazing."

Leslie's mom, Suzanne, emailed back, "Congratulations. What an awesome achievement. I'm so proud of both of you." So, it'll slowly sink in as people ask about our trip. We obviously didn't just hike 73 days without a day off so that we could hear people congratulate us . . . but it's nice to hear when someone at least has a vague notion of what it takes to do this kind of thing.

It's a weird feeling, that getting to the end of this trail was just a moment in time. Just a pinpoint on a long 73-day continuum. And then we immediately move into the next moment and it's sort of like the entire trip never happened. We get to the official end of the trail, look at the little ceramic tile design on the ground, take some photos, throw my stinky rotting hiking shoes in a garbage can, and then a guy offered us a ride to the train station, and now we're on the train heading to London. Tomorrow we'll fly home to Indiana, and on Saturday we'll wake up in our bed and it'll feel like we never left. Goldie will need to be let out to go potty, Gizmo will act like she's starving, and Gabby will be laying on the back of the couch looking out the window. And the moments will continue, and the rest of life will go on.

When we first arrived at the end of the trail, at around 2:20pm (we started out at 7:45am this morning), there was a family . . . a mom, dad, and two boys who were standing there and reading the words on the end-point monument. They weren't really sure what it was and were reading about the trail. And then we walked up with our dirty backpacks, and soaking wet shoes and socks, and said we'd just finished hiking the entire 870-mile trail that they were reading about. They were kind of astonished that we'd just walked up.

We asked them to take several pictures, and they asked lots of questions. The guy's mom and dad were named Jon and Leslie, which was kind of funny. So, they shared our final moments on the trail with us. Just like some random people shared our tears of joy when we finished hiking the Southwest Coast Path in 2015.

And then this older guy that I already mentioned, who was checking around for a geo-cache, came up and offered us a ride to the train station. So, we unceremoniously peeled off our soaking wet shoes and socks, and threw them in the nearest garbage can. That was liberating.

When we arrived at the Chepstow station, the train to Newport was just pulling up, so we bought our tickets and sprinted onto the train. And all of the sudden we were heading home. Just like that.

We wanted to get going early this morning since we had 14.5 miles to hike, plus a four-hour train ride. So, we were up at 6am and having breakfast across the street at a little local diner at 6:45am. We decided to get breakfast sandwiches to-go, since neither of us was hungry that early. The breakfast lady was super nice and made us two great egg, bacon, and sausage sandwiches, and two tuna sandwiches for lunch. Our taxi came and as we were about to leave, the breakfast lady said, "Here, please pick out two bags of crisps for free." And then, "Your trip won't be complete without these." And she handed me two big chocolate creamy deserts. What a great way to start our final day.

The shocker of the day happened on our way back to London. We ran onto that first train heading to Chepstow, which actually traveled 25 miles in the "wrong" direction away from London, to the larger city of Newport. At the Newport Station, we had a 40-minute wait for our next train to London's Paddington Station. About 10 minutes before the train was supposed to arrive, I went to find a bathroom. About five minutes before our departing train arrived, I came back to tell Leslie where the bathroom was. About one minute before our train arrived, everyone waiting at Track #3 stood up to get ready to board the train that was now pulling into the station.

When the train arrived, I waited until everyone else had boarded, and then grabbed both of our packs to get a seat on the train. No sign of Leslie. I dropped both packs on two seats and went back to the train door to watch for her. I was starting to panic, because no one was left on the platform outside, and I couldn't get the door open. I finally asked someone how to open the door, and they said that once the conductor closes the door and the train is about to leave, you have to reach through the window to the outside door handle and open it from the outside. Which I did.

I looked up and down the platform. No sign of Leslie. The conductors yelled at me from a couple of cars down, "Get in the train. We're leaving." I yelled back, "My wife isn't on the train. I need to go grab my bags and get off." So, I ran back in, grabbed the packs, and just as I was jumping off the train, Leslie comes walking up the aisle from the next car. She'd seen the train about to leave, and jumped into the final car, and was walking through the cars to find me. Phew!

It wasn't until after we'd both caught our breath and were heading towards London, that we realized that Leslie had no cell phone, no money, no credit cards, and no train ticket with her. Everything was either in my pockets or in our packs. If I hadn't seen her at the last second, like if she'd gotten on the train but was still a few cars back, I'd have gotten off with everything, and she'd be on the train with no phone, no ticket, no money, and no way to communicate with me. Or, if I hadn't been able to get that door open, and she hadn't made it on the train yet, I'd be heading to London with Leslie stuck back in Newport, with no way to call each other. I just said to Leslie, "What would we have done?" And she keeps replying,

"Shush. I don't want to talk about it."

I finally convinced her that we need a plan for situations like this in the future, which included neither of us ever being without our phones and a little bit of money. So, we came up with a plan for next time. Yikes. What an exciting end to our hike.

It was a three-hour train ride to London's Paddington Station, where this whole adventure began. Then another train to Heathrow. And then another to Terminal 4 where our Premier Hotel was located. We checked into a U.K. hotel one last time, had dinner and a drink in a U.K. restaurant one last time, and went to bed.

We flew all day on November 3rd to Minneapolis and then on to Indianapolis. Tyler and Dana were there to meet us. And we were back home in Bloomington, reunited with Goldie, Gizmo, and Gabby, and in bed by 1:30am that next morning.

And now, a day later, it feels like we were never even in Wales. How does this happen?

While we were hiking for two and a half months, it felt like we'd been doing it forever, and we could barely remember when we'd started the hike. And now that it's over, it feels like it all went by in the blink of an eye. Like it was just yesterday that we had our bags packed and were heading to the airport. That was in August, 78 days ago!!

The experience of time passing is so relative. Relative to our emotional state; relative to our thought processes; and relative to how we choose to experience the moment we are in.

Leslie's Journal Entry:

Last Day

TRAIL GUIDES
& WEBSITES

Websites

www.walescoastpath.gov.uk

www.walescoastpath.co.uk

Guidebooks

There are numerous guidebooks and maps for individual sections of the Wales Coast Path that provide suggested day- and week-end-long hikes. But, for those who are planning a through-hike of the entire trail, these are the books you need.

Wales Coast Path Official Guide is a seven-book series of excellent and very detailed trail guides and maps. This set of guidebooks are indispensable for any through-hiker. Each book covers one of the key sections of the path. Together, they cover the entire 1400-kilometer/870-mile route, from Chester to Chepstow. Each handy, pocket-sized book contains everything you need to plan and walk the route. Features include distance charts, day-walk sections, detailed route descriptions, reliable local information, enhanced Ordnance Survey mapping, and plenty of superb color photos. The guidebooks are published and available to buy from the Northern Eye Books website: www.norterneyebooks.co.uk.

The seven section guidebooks are:

North Wales Coast by Lorna Jenner – Chester to Bangor, 125km/80 miles

Isle of Anglesey Coast Path by Carl Rogers – Isle of Anglesey Coast, 210km/130 miles

Llyn Peninsula by Carl Roges and Tony Bowerman – Bangor to Porthmadog, 180km/110 miles

Snowdonia & Ceredigion Coast by Vivienne Crow – Porthmadog to Cardigan, 213km/132 miles

Pembrokeshire by Vivienne Crow – Cardigan to Amroth, 300km/186 miles

Carmarthen Bay & Gower by Harri Garrod Roberts – Tenby to Swansea, 208km/130 miles

South Wales Coast by Dennis & Jan Kelsall – Swansea to Chepstow, 180km/110 miles

Walking The Wales Coast Path (*Llwybr Arfordir Cymru*), by Paddy Dillon and published by Cicerone, Milnthrope, U.K. (2016), is a single-book guide to walking the whole Wales Coast Path—870 miles, the length of Wales from Chester to Chepstow, including Anglesey—described in 57 stages and grouped into eight regions.

The Wales Coast Path: A Practical Guide for Walkers, by Chris Goddard and Katharine Evans and published by St. David's Press (2020), is a guidebook and essential companion to the entire path for both the serious long-distance walker and for day-trippers who wish to tackle the path one stage at a time. The guidebook presents the complete Wales Coast Path via 73 manageable walks of approximately nine to 15 miles each; provides easy-to-follow route descriptions and contains over 80 hand-drawn maps; is full of additional information on sites of historical, geological, and wildlife interest; suggests alternative routes that enable short visits to additional key locations just off the official Coast Path; and enables walkers to maximize local amenities and services such as public transport, car parking, and accommodation options such as camp sites and B&Bs.

JONATHAN WUNROW is a new grandparent, parent, husband, adventurer, grant writer, cabin builder, beer brewer, Tribal advocate, and Green Bay Packer fanatic who occasionally finds time to plan and enjoy adventures around the world.

In addition to pursuing his passion for climbing many of the highest peaks in the Western Hemisphere, he has also hiked the 2,650-mile Pacific Crest Trail, paddled the Mississippi River, climbed Kilimanjaro with his son Seth, hiked the 870-mile Wales Coast Path and the 630-mile Southwest Coast Path with his wife Leslie, and has enjoyed cycling, hiking, climbing, and beach-sitting adventures in dozens of countries all over the world.

After living and raising his son in Sitka, Alaska, for 16 years, the author now resides in Bloomington, Indiana, with his amazing and supportive wife Leslie, and visits has grandson Arlo in Michigan whenever he can.

Wunrow is also the author of *Adventure Inward: A Risk Taker's Book of Quotes*, *High Points: A Climber's Guide to Central America*, and *High Points: A Climber's Guide to South America, Part I*.

Printed in Great Britain
by Amazon